THE NEW CONQUEROR

Book Two in the *Revelation in Our Time* Trilogy

Hugh Shelbourne

Innovo Publishing

Published by
Innovo Publishing, LLC
www.innovopublishing.com
1-888-546-2111

Providing Full-Service Publishing Services for
Christian Authors, Artists & Organizations: Hardbacks, Paperbacks,
eBooks, Audiobooks, Music & Videos

THE NEW CONQUEROR
Book Two in the *Revelation in Our Time* Trilogy
Copyright © 2011 by Hugh Shelbourne
All rights reserved.

Scripture is taken from the Revised Standard Version of the Bible. Copyright ©1952 [2nd Edition, 1971]
by the Division of Christian Education of the National Council of the Churches of Christ
in the United States of America. Used by permission. All rights reserved.

Library of Congress Control Number: 2011929474
ISBN 13: 978-1-936076-77-2
ISBN 10: 1-936076-77-2

Cover Design & Interior Layout: Innovo Publishing, LLC

Printed in the United States of America
U.S. Printing History

First Edition: June 2011

THE NEW CONQUEROR

Helmet of salvation I John 2:12

Breastplate of righteousness Romans 1:16,17

Sword of the Spirit Hebrews 4:12

Shield of faith Ephesians 2:8

Loins girded with truth John 17:17

Feet shod with the gospel of peace Romans 10:15

*** STAND THEREFORE
*** AND PRAY AT ALL TIMES IN THE SPIRIT,
WITH ALL PRAYER AND SUPPLICATION
*** KEEP ALERT WITH ALL PERSEVERANCE
(Ephesians 6:13-19)

*** HERE IS A CALL FOR THE PATIENCE
AND ENDURANCE OF THE SAINTS
(Revelation 13:10)

*** HE WHO ENDURES TO THE END
WILL BE SAVED
(Matthew 24:13)

TABLE OF CONTENTS

INTRODUCTION

On a lovely, sunny morning in 1994, in the troubled nation of Rwanda, a horrible madness broke out. The people awoke to hear their radios blaring a call to the Hutu tribe. The summons was to rise up and slaughter their Tutsi neighbours. No one knows for sure how many were killed over the next terrible weeks, but approximately one million people met their death and many others were maimed for life.

It is true that this did not come out of the blue. For years there had been a deliberate campaign of political propaganda drawing on the latent hatred that exists between all tribes as a means to get permanent control of the country. Competition between the tribes for domination was nothing new. It had been going on for generations.

Later that year my wife, Juliet, and I went into Rwanda from neighbouring Uganda. We went in with returning Christian refugees from past pogroms whose families had left thirty years before. By the time we got there, the killing was over and the RPF (Rwanda Patriotic Front) Army, mostly Tutsi, was regaining control. The villages were largely empty and Kigali was a ghost town because so many inhabitants had either been killed or had fled for their lives.

Going into the country was an eerie experience. There was a hush on the land, because normal life had been suspended. Those who were left were in a state of shock. The graves were still fresh and there were many bodies as yet unburied. Everyone had an unbelievable story to tell. All had lost family members. In many cases, entire families had been wiped out. The land was soaked with blood and I was reminded of God's words to Cain, *"Listen! Your brother's blood cries out to me from the ground"* (Genesis 4:10, NIV).

As a Christian and a Bible teacher, the whole experience presented me with a tremendous challenge, for Rwanda is not a pagan nation. Statistics say that 80 percent of the people are "committed Christians." The churches of all denominations are full and thriving. There is sound documentary evidence that during the last seventy years there have been at least three "Holy Spirit revivals" sweeping the nation! We were witnessing the killing of untold thousands of Christians by other Christians, many claiming to be "Spirit filled." Testimonies tell of church leaders at all levels who betrayed and killed members of their own flock. Grandfathers and fathers killed their own family members without mercy, often in obscene and brutal ways. Neighbours who had lived together and even intermarried now took their pangas* and turned on their companions in a frenzy of blood lust.

How could this be? That was the question Juliet and I were faced with. I had ministered the Word to others for twenty-five years. What had the Word to show me in this situation? I could not walk around it or

---

* A panga is a broad, heavy African knife, keenly sharp and used as a hacking tool or, in this case, as a terrible weapon.

away from it: here I was trying to teach the Bible to Africans and yet here before my eyes was the naked reality of what is in the human heart. But these were *Christians*. Christians or not, I realised there was something deep within them that should not be there.

I now went through a process that took many long weeks. I knew that I could not go on without somehow finding the answer to that question: how could this be?

We had made our home in the hills of western Uganda. Juliet created a lovely garden there. In a corner of the garden there is a particular rock where I would sit for hours on end. When the sun became too overpowering, an adjacent stream with a waterfall cooled me off. I could look up to the heights of the adjoining hills or down the valley where unending streams of people walked up and down the road going about their business. It is a scene repeated all over Africa.

As I pondered the appalling images that had impressed themselves upon my mind, the thing that shocked me most was that in spite of all the years of teaching and churchgoing to which those Christians had been exposed, murder was still in their hearts.

But then came a bigger shock! I came to understand that it was not only Rwanda that was pressing on my mind. It was *me*! God said, *"What about **your** heart, Hugh?"*

It did not take long for me to acknowledge a dreadful truth: given the circumstances I could find it in *me* to kill. Me, a sixty-year-old Bible teacher, proud of my faith, proud of my ministry, proud of my family, proud of my achievements in life, and proud of my Englishness; I, too, could kill just as those Africans had done.

In 1 John 3:15, John wrote: *"He who hates his brother is a murderer already"* (NIV). Jesus said that murder comes out of the heart (Matthew 15:19). These familiar words from the New Testament were the beginning of a deeply penetrating process of investigation into my own condition. I knew that, like the people John and Jesus had in mind, I too had a heart problem. I knew that behind murder lies hatred. But why is hatred in *my* heart and how do I get it out?

I realise, that, like love, hatred has many shades to it. We do not all go about with murderous intent to kill others because our hatred is relatively benign and hidden by social protocol. However, when cause is given, that unsuspected hatred can suddenly rise up and take over. We say hurtful things, we become violent, we lose control of our own behaviour, and we wish hurt and even death to others. "I could have *killed* him/her!" is a common expression in society; everyone understands it very well and even sympathises with it when heard!

I know full well that Jesus commanded us to love one another as he has loved us. How then is the hatred in me to be replaced by that love? As a husband, father, and grandfather I had thought that I loved quite well. Indeed I was rather proud of both my self-control and my relationships. But now I began to see that things were not as I had thought. There was something in me that certainly was not love, and I did not know how it got there or how to get rid of it. Furthermore, I saw that the love of which I was so proud, was *conditional* love: I turned it on and off according to circumstances. I knew that God, my Father *is* love—and he wants his sons, not just *to* love, but also to *be* love. Even after nearly fifty years as a Christian I knew this was a dimension well beyond my personal experience. Something was missing.

Something had been missing from my ministry too. It was no wonder that people were not changed through my ministry! They may have been *blessed*, yes, but had they been changed? No they had not, and for very good reason. I myself had not been changed by what I taught, so why should they be changed? There was something here that I had never understood and I needed to understand it before I could move forward.

Clue number one came from the realisation that the first murder in the Bible is Cain's killing of his brother Abel. Cain's terrible crime and the birth of Seth are the only recorded incidents of Adam and Eve's family life after they were expelled from the Garden of Eden. The murder of Abel is therefore of profound significance for us. God deliberately uses it to show us what is in man's heart as a direct consequence of the Fall.

When the Holy Spirit left Adam, characteristics of the loving God in him were replaced by characteristics of Satan. Hatred was one, but only one of many. Scripture uses the word "iniquity" as a collective term for satanic characteristics. Here is the key that unlocked the conundrum for me.

Through Ezekiel 28:15, God reveals a remarkable truth about Satan: "*You were perfect in your ways from the day you were created, 'til iniquity was found in you*" (NKJV).

Satan (the Hebrew means "adversary" or "enemy") had once been known as Lucifer, the Son of Dawn (the name Lucifer means "shining one"). But through his rebellion against God he was cast out of heaven.

As it was for Satan, so it was for Adam. In that day of rebellion known as "the Fall," Adam was put out of Eden. But more than that, the son of God (Adam) had become the son of Satan. In consequence of this we are all born with the same problem. I understood all too well that this was painfully true of me. If it is not dealt with, we remain helpless to overcome Satan in our personal lives and relationships and it is impossible for us to be changed into the likeness of Jesus.

God had taken my wife and me to Africa to reveal something to me. In my search for understanding of my own problem I had at last discovered iniquity, the poison of the soul. There is no antidote. It can never be cleaned up; it must be put to death. Unless it is put to death it will grow and infest every part of our being. It is a killer and it must be killed.

This book tracks the path that Jesus has pioneered. He has blazed the trail, making it possible for us all to walk in his footsteps. It is orthodox Christian teaching but some of it has been forgotten in the churches at large. Juliet and I give testimony to the power of God's Word to change us as we take up the cross daily. As we were changed, God began to change others around us.

Jesus promised that those who hunger and thirst after righteousness will be filled (Matthew 5:6). Filled with what? Obviously we shall be filled with what we hunger and thirst for—righteousness! Righteousness in place of present unrighteousness. What a promise! *But, that desperate hunger and thirst had to come first.*

Once we had understood for ourselves how this happens, Juliet and I saw other believers being changed, marriages being changed, and families being changed—often overnight. We had discovered that a kind of tribalism is rooted deep in us all. Hatred of others lies at its heart: just one of the many vicious expressions of iniquity.

In Ezekiel 33, God speaks of the work of his "watchmen." Jesus took up the theme in Mark 13:32–37, calling all Christians to be "watchmen" for his soon coming. Watchmen are responsible for preparing themselves and their loved ones for the Day of his coming.

To be ready, we need to be saved *and* to be sanctified. How can we do it? It took us two years in Africa to recognize our need and then to find the answer. The comprehensive revelation of both was to be found in the Scriptures. At last I found it!

DECEIVED AND DYING:
MAN'S UNSEEN BLACK HOLE

A deceiver's first purpose is to gain the confidence of the potential victim he wishes to deceive. He needs to be disarming, charming, and impressive in order to gain his victim's trust, but beneath the surface is a ruthless thief whose aim is to steal or destroy for his own illicit ends.

The nature of deception is that the "deceived" does not realize he has a problem until it is too late. To achieve his goal, the deceiver has to convince the deceived that he is speaking truth, or at least that he is not lying. In deception, appearance counts for everything. The deceiver must make a good first impression and then he must have a smooth, confident presentation of his story. Flattery and false friendship are the frequent prelude to fraud, with the suggestion that what is being proposed is in the best interests of the listener. The deceiver must appear to be indifferent to the outcome. It is often the case that the victim is hearing things that are agreeable to him and wanting to believe them if possible; he suspends taking the measures by which he would usually protect himself. Today, we may call it "spin" or "being economical with the truth," but anything less than the whole truth is deception.

The ages past have thrown up many claimants for the title of the "Worst Tyrant in History," but none can match the arch deceiver, the devil himself, who is described in Genesis 3:1 as, *"more crafty than any of the wild animals that the Lord God had made"* (NIV). The devil's breathtaking audacity goes largely unrecognised by those who should know better, even today.

The Bible calls the devil the *"deceiver of the whole world"* (Revelation 12:9). On three occasions, Jesus called him the *"ruler of this world"* (John 12:31, 14:30, 16:11) and John tells us that the *"whole world is in the power of the evil one"* (1 John 5:19). So it is clear, according to the Bible, that Satan rules the whole of this world we live in and he does so by deception.

Who amongst us really believes such a staggering statement? The astonishing fact is that by his deceptions Satan has achieved almost complete control over thousands of years of the world's known history. Satan controls our world and is therefore its master, yet most people, including believers, are in total ignorance of this fact. This is no recent phenomenon: such ignorance of Satan's power and position has always dogged mankind.

Satan manipulates the minds of men by his manoeuvres, dominating them with lies and deception. Through these means he has succeeded in discounting the revelation of the Bible, ousting God as the great Creator who is to be worshiped by his creatures, and encouraging man to believe the incredible lie of evolution together with other absurd, pseudo-scientific theories.

In order to maintain his precious independence, rebellious man is always desperate to find acceptable alternatives to the claims of the Almighty God who is revealed by the Bible. Man wants to escape the fearful conclusion that there is a holy God who dispenses justice. Man prefers to accept theories of an accidental evolution of life as an explanation of the wondrous creation of which we are a part. He chooses to believe that the perfectly ordered universe we occupy is the result of a haphazard explosion in a void!

Man longs to find evidence of life on some other planet. He searches almost desperately for evidence to support the flimsy theories that life on earth is not unique. The Bible shows us otherwise.

Man prefers to live a life with no ultimate purpose rather than accept the exciting claims made in the Bible that show each person as known to God, and that he has a purpose for us and has given our lives an eternal dimension.

What is this devilish deception that still has such power over mankind? What kind of lie can so win the hearts and minds of untold millions against the evidence of God revealed in creation and in the Bible?

This lie has tenacious power to cling to the minds of men in spite of the catalogue of disasters they see all around them. An all-pervading blindness seems to prevent people from seeing what lies behind the chaos, anarchy, and degeneration of our world. People are incapable of seeing and believing the truth because they are gripped by this great lie.

Throughout the violent, bloody history of our world mankind, with rare exceptions, has consistently and deliberately rejected the authority of the one living God who is the Father of Jesus Christ. For over 2000 years man has refused to accept the legitimate authority of the risen Jesus, preferring to live under the lie he has been told rather than the truth of what God says in the Bible. What is this lie and where does it come from?

Although we can and should work to discover the answer to these questions, we will not enjoy the answer when we find it, for it is most dreadfully painful to our pride. The Jews of Jesus' time did not enjoy the truth that he revealed to them throughout his ministry. They saw themselves as uniquely chosen by God under the Old Covenant, not realizing that in every dispensation of God's grace to men he has required them to have faith in his given Word. Being born a Jew was not enough. It was a good beginning, but thereafter life was to be lived by faith under the terms of God's covenant.

On one occasion, a group of Jews was arguing with Jesus about their status as natural descendants of Abraham. They had expressed a grudging admiration for Jesus' teaching because it was consistent with Hebrew Scriptures. But they prided themselves on their position as Abraham's sons and were claiming a special relationship with God based upon their lineage and their religious practices. Jesus' words must have shaken them to the core. What he said immediately exposed Satan's true nature and the basis of his relationship with all mankind, including unfaithful Jewry. In John 8:42–44, Jesus said:

> *"If God were your Father, you would love me, for I proceeded and came forth from God; I came not of my own accord but he sent me. Why do you not understand what I say? It is because you cannot bear to hear my word. You are of your father the devil, and your will is to do your father's desires. He was a murderer from the beginning, and has nothing to do with the truth, because there is no truth in him. When he lies (lit: when he speaks The Lie), he speaks according to his own nature, for he is a liar and the father of lies (lit: the father of it)."*

English usage is defective in that while we have a noun that is inclusive of all truth, namely *"the* truth," there is no English word to denote the whole body of *un*truth that exists. But when Jesus spoke of "the lie," he meant precisely that: the whole body of untruth that exists. This is the meaning of the original Hebrew Jesus used and that was translated into Greek.

Jesus shows us that for all the Jews' religious practices and pride in their birth, there was a connection between them and Satan! Our Lord actually likened it to a father-child relationship. We find that Satan is the source of "the lie" and those who live their lives under "the lie" demonstrate that they are Satan's offspring. Jesus points to the power of "the lie," as delivered by Satan, to give life to its adherents in a similar way that the truth of Jesus' words gives life to the believer.

Of course the life given by "the lie" is of a different quality from that given by "the truth," but we must remember that these religious people were deceived, as are all people dominated by religion. Far from being sons of God as they claim, Jesus shocks them by telling them that they are sons of the devil. This was not because they were particularly bad, or worse than any others, but because they, living by "the lie" and not by "the truth" that Jesus had come to bring them, were living in darkness with no insight into their true condition.

By extension it may then be said that all human beings are born sons of Satan. This is not in the biological sense, but in the sense that Jesus used the term. All take after the devil because they inevitably share his nature until they are set free by "the truth" as true sons of God. John confirms this in his first epistle:

> "*He who commits sin is of the devil; for the devil has sinned from the beginning. The reason the Son of God appeared was to destroy the works of the devil. No one born of God commits sin; for God's nature abides in him and he cannot sin because he is born of God. By this it may be seen who are children of God, and who are the children of the devil: whoever does not do right is not of God, nor he who does not love his brother*" (1 John 3:8–10).

But it was not always like this. To understand how the change came about we have to examine the events in the Garden of Eden where the first and fatal deception of man took place.

In amongst all the other trees in the Garden of Eden stood a very strange fruit tree, called the Tree of Knowledge of Good and Evil. God had placed it there to provide a test for Adam and Eve. God respects our integrity, so in every age he presents man with an option. Either man can live under God's Word by faith, or he can choose to ignore God's Word and live by his own choices. The tree represented such an opportunity for choice to Adam and Eve. Genesis 3:5 makes it clear that in rebelling against God by eating the luscious forbidden fruit, Adam expected to attain not only independence from God but also a far higher status than God had given him hitherto (even to become like God himself). He and Eve would open up a whole new world of previously hidden knowledge, making available to them things both good and evil.

An intriguing modern parallel may be seen on the Internet. Promising vastly increased access to knowledge of good, it yet lures countless numbers to secretly access devastating pornographic and other unclean material.

To be tempted is not in itself evil: rather it is a test (after all, Jesus was tempted in the Judean Wilderness), but if something unclean lies hidden in the heart, temptation calls it forth.

James gives us light on the value of this tree. He writes in James 1:12–15:

> "*Blessed is the man who endures trial, for when he has stood the test, he will receive the crown of life which God has promised to those who love him. Let no one say when he is tempted, "I am tempted by God"; for God cannot be tempted by evil and he himself tempts no one; each person is tempted when he is lured and enticed by his own desire. Then desire when it has conceived gives birth to sin; and sin when it is full grown brings forth death.*"

God had specifically warned Adam as to the consequences of eating the fruit: "*In the day you eat of its fruit you shall surely die*" (Genesis 2:17). We know that Satan came to Eve with a lie directly contradicting God's Word.

"*You shall not surely die,*" he said and then added a promise of his own, "*for you will be as God, knowing good and evil.*" That too, was a lie, for Adam was much less like God after he had eaten the fruit than he was before. But these two lies together constitute the lie by which Satan has deceived all mankind. Its working is the same for each of us, as it was at first for Eve.

First of all, Eve was enchanted by the lie. The process is there in Scripture. Eve saw that "*the fruit was good for food, and that it was a delight to the eyes, and was to be desired to make one wise*" (Genesis 3:6). The process is stated as a principle in 1 John 2:16. Desire for the forbidden fruit was planted in Eve's heart. Now she was on dangerous territory, thinking thoughts in contradiction to God's words.

Overwhelmed by the occasion and by the appearance of the glorious creature addressing her (surely such a one would not tell her lies!), she took and ate. In just the same way, Satan has enchanted and entertained man's vanity ever since and with the same disastrous consequences.

In the first moment of eating, nothing happened and Eve assumed that she was vindicated in doing what she had done. So she did what we all do—she went to involve her mate in her foolishness. "Look! It's okay; God did not really mean what he said about the tree! I met this wonderful creature and he assured me that God was only tricking us because he wanted to prevent us from knowing as much as he knows!"

We know that Adam's case was different from Eve's. Eve had been well and truly deceived by Satan, but Adam was *not* deceived by Eve's excited account and he realized immediately the full implications of what she had done. Adam's actions were not under the influence of deception; they were deliberate. Adam deliberately rebelled against God. He chose to disobey God rather than lose the beautiful wife who was flesh of his flesh and bone of his bone. By his cowardly action Adam failed God, failed his wife, and failed his race. He sinned, and in consequence the eyes of both of them were opened and they knew what they had done, understanding something of its appalling consequences. But it was too late for regret; —there was no way back. In an instant their glory had gone. The Holy Spirit had gone. Their love had gone. Their innocence had gone. Their life with God had gone—they were indeed dead. Father had gone. They opted for "the lie" and now Satan would be their spiritual parent.

We must not fall into the trap of thinking that this deception was a simple matter. It was the fruit of genius: nothing had been better calculated. In Ezekiel 28, we find a fascinating and revealing prophecy through which God exposes Satan (Lucifer) and his fall from heaven and ultimate destruction. The linkage of Satan with the king of Tyre in this chapter is curious. Commentators are not clear about it and some actually link the king with Adam! However a closer reading of verses 11–19 makes it obvious that the king of Tyre is a deliberate pseudonym for Satan.

Ezekiel says: "*You were the signet of perfection, full of wisdom and perfect in beauty*" (Ezekiel 28:12b). So the deception of Eve was perpetrated by a superior being who was calling upon everything he knew in order that he might interfere with the Creator's purpose in creation. This affords us further insight into what took place, for in Ezekiel 28:17 God addresses Satan through the prophet: "*Your heart was proud because of your beauty; you corrupted your wisdom for the sake of your splendour (lit: shining).*"

Because of his unique beauty and exceptional wisdom Lucifer was lifted up in his heart and at some point had decided that he could be equal to God (Isaiah 14:12–14). He was the first to take the path of all sinners described by James in his little letter (James 1:13–15). Having conceived in his heart the desire to be equal to God, Lucifer did not resist it and his rebellion became inevitable. The heavenly creature created by God to shine with heaven's brightest splendour became the darkest adversary, the enemy of God.

The desperate, proud ambition of Lucifer to be God is identified for us as "iniquity" (Ezekiel 28:15 and 18[KJV]). It is "the lie" in the heart, and its immediate and inevitable consequences are:

- "dishonest trade" (NIV) (i.e. greed for gain: covetousness which equals idolatry) rather than serving God (which equals worship)

- violence (hatred/murder of all opposition) The first expression of Satan's iniquity was probably developed in the negotiations, threats, and promises by which he deceived one third of all the angels in heaven into following him in his rebellion (Revelation 12:4).

On the day that Lucifer, the great angel that Isaiah called "*Day Star, Son of Dawn*" (Isaiah 14:12 [NIV]), was cast out of heaven he needed somewhere to exercise his chosen independence from God. The created earth was his only option. To take control of the earth, Satan would need to subvert Adam to his will. Adam was God's chosen creature to whom he had given dominion over his creation on the earth. The stakes were high. Satan knew his strategy would certainly need to be subtle. He needed a quick, complete, and permanent victory over Adam to gain mastery of the earth. The Tree of Knowledge of Good and Evil, deliberately put in place by God, provided his opportunity. It was the one spot in the Garden where Adam and Eve were vulnerable.

Now that he was separated from Almighty God whom he had served for so long, Satan fully understood the meaning of death. If he could achieve the separation of Adam from his Creator, this would serve his purposes perfectly. *He* would become Adam's God, effectively manipulating him from behind the scenes. Satan's lust for worship and acceptance would be fully gratified. It would not be necessary for Adam to praise Satan openly—to sing hymns and songs or even to pray to him. Obedience was enough. Satan would gorge himself on Adam's unwitting worship.

Inevitably Satan came offering to Eve exactly the same powerful and corrosive temptation by which he himself had been corrupted. The first stage of being separated from God is to deny his absolute right to sovereignty, thus reducing him to our level. The entertainment of that evil thought leads subtly and directly to the second stage: complete separation from him, for if God has any equal he is no longer God.

When Adam took and ate the fruit it was symbolic of "digesting the lie" both he and Eve had accepted from the master deceiver. Abandoning "the truth" under which they had lived, he and Eve imbibed the subtle determination to be as God, deciding good and evil. Rebellion inevitably brought death. As Satan, they too were immediately separated from God and put out of his presence. The Holy Spirit had indwelt Adam and Eve from the beginning; now he left them and instead of the pure atmosphere of heaven they breathed the foul, stale breath of iniquity. The Word of God had been their unseen guide, but now, in the independence of their awakened pride, they had the freedom to choose their own way.

Satan's promises were soon proved to be empty. All too late Adam and Eve discovered the lamentable reality of their new state. Far from being like God who knows the end from the beginning, they had no power to foresee the consequences of their choices and no power to implement their choices when they had made them! Every moment they were subject to entirely new and unrecognised pressures. Their own thoughts, feelings, and emotions were no substitute for the certainties of God's Word, and they had the atmospheric pressures generated by the prince of the power of the air to cope with. Satan could pull their strings whenever he wanted. They knew what was good but they could not do it in an untainted way. Knowing evil, they found themselves doing it even when they did not want to! Gone was the Holy Spirit's power and they no longer lived in the dimension of the heavenly places—God's spirit world.

Most of the time they did not know what to do. They were tied to their environment. Without love, they hated and would kill. Without love, they would lust and be unfaithful. Without truth, they would lie and deceive each other. **C**riticism, **R**esentment, **A**nger, **B**itterness and **S**elf-pity against God and one another filled their hearts and overwhelmed them (**CRABS** is a useful mnemonic for remembering some of these things!).

The prophet Jeremiah says, *"The heart is deceitful above all things and desperately corrupt; who can understand it?"* (Jeremiah 17:9). Even their own heart, the previous seat and source of their Spirit-filled life, now deceived them. Their generosity had turned into a spiritual black hole, sucking everything in and giving nothing out willingly. They longed for approval and acceptance but, being in competition, could not give it to one another. They had become like their spiritual father, Satan. Adam's iniquity, derived from Satan, would be passed down from generation to generation forever, beginning with Cain.

This is how we are all born—with iniquity in our hearts. It has been called "original sin." This is man's problem—the unacknowledged sickness of the human heart. Fallen man is in a desperate state. *"You are of your father the devil and your will is to do your father's desires,"* Jesus had said (John 8:44). Can that statement really be true of us all? Oh yes, and history is its demonstration. This has been the unequivocal truth of man's condition ever since the Fall.

God made the situation quite clear when he spoke to Cain immediately before the killing of his brother Abel. God said, *"If you do well will you not be accepted? And if you do not do well, sin (iniquity) is couching at the door, its desire is for you and you must overcome it"* (Genesis 4:7). Incredibly, Cain did not permit himself to be affected by God's gracious warning; there was no repentance and he went ahead and killed his brother in cold blood.

What was true for Cain is true for us all. Acknowledging it, however, is a different matter. Our pride (another expression of iniquity) is affronted by such a sweeping proposition. Even Christians are so used to thinking at the Tree of Knowledge that it has become ingrained and they refuse to face the truth. "I've been a Christian for years—a pillar of the local church. What you say simply cannot be true!"

By claiming God's right to determine good and evil, we identify some good in ourselves. We might also identify some evil. We might be persuaded to identify that evil as being a manifestation of iniquity, but we are not so easily persuaded to identify the *good* as being a manifestation of iniquity! Even in exchange for a new life promised by Jesus! And yet Isaiah identifies the truth about our so-called goodness when he writes, *". . . all our righteous acts are like filthy rags . . . and like the wind, our [iniquities] sweep us away"* (Isaiah 64:6).

(This includes all *religious* belief and practice that is not unequivocally the expression of God's Word. That is what so offended the religious Jews when Jesus exposed them (John 8:42–44). They imagined that Judaism was acceptable to God without the practical application of faith. They were wrong. We face the same challenge as we review our Christian beliefs and practices. If they are not according to the Word of God, they have their source in Satan's purposes and not God's!)

Paul confirms this in Romans 7:18–19. And here is the rub: until and unless we are convicted of this truth about our condition, there can be no real repentance because we would not be dealing with the root of the problem—the iniquity in our heart, lurking at the door like some dark beast patiently waiting for an opportunity to rise up. What Jesus said is "the truth." We are sons of the devil living under the lie. If we cannot see our problem, then we cannot receive the cure.

Living now in the harsh and unyielding environment of a cursed world, we are a deceived and deceiving people, ruled by an unseen monster inside and the hosts of wickedness outside. Man in his blindness, believing he sees, is lost in spiritual darkness. His mind and heart are hostile to God. He enjoys the lusts of the flesh.

We are all born in this condition, completely subservient to the ruler of this world and helpless to help ourselves. Stubbornly refusing the revelation of God's Word and its authority over our lives, we foolishly await a judgment in which the evidence presented will not be how well we carried out the duties of a religious life, the correctness of our doctrinal beliefs or the record of our charity. Rather, the evidence will be the accumulated iniquity that is in our hearts after a lifetime of living only for ourselves. That evidence will speak only too eloquently. We shall be able to offer no excuses to improve our case and there will be no one there to plead our cause. The Lord spoke of this judgement in Jeremiah 17:10: *"I the Lord search the mind and try the heart, to give to every man according to his ways, according to the fruit of his doings."*

Because God is eminently gracious and outstandingly patient in the face of great provocation, there is still time to find him. But to do so we must hunger and thirst for righteousness rather than knowledge, and we must come to him desiring "the truth," which can only be found if we first turn away from "the lie." There must be this deep, burning desire for deliverance from iniquity. *The Spirit and the Bride say, "Come." And let him who hears say, "Come." And let him who is thirsty come, let him who desires take the water of life without price* (Revelation 22:17).

You can come—today!

THE BLOOD RANSOM IS ENOUGH

There is a wonderful scene in Revelation chapter 5 where John stands in God's throne room surrounded by the heavenly hosts. They are all caught up in worshiping God. In a unique revelation, John sees God holding a great scroll with seven seals upon it. We are not told what the scroll is, but just as in our culture we have written title deeds of land or property ownership; we can deduce that the scroll is probably the title deed to the earth that belongs only in the hands of its rightful owner.

At the moment, Satan is the ruler of the world, but his rule is not legitimate, for he usurped the dominion originally given to Adam by a ruse and a deception. How can that dominion be reclaimed?

Legally, a legitimate claimant to the title must be found. Only he has the right to take the scroll and open it. If there is no such claimant, the world must go on in its desperate darkness and God's plan in creation will remain unfulfilled.

Aware of this tragedy, John weeps that there appears to be no one qualified to take the scroll from God's hand. But then one of the twenty-four elders comes to him, comforts him, and assures him that all is well because there *is* such a claimant. The elder's words have profound importance in providing an understanding of the transaction that is taking place here. Someone has come forward claiming the right to the title deeds of the earth. It is Jesus. Jesus Christ is both the Lion of the Tribe of Judah (fulfilling the prophecy of Genesis 49:8–10) and is also the Root of David (fulfilling the prophecy of Isaiah 11:1–10).

Because he was born of a human mother, Jesus is a son of Adam. He is of the lineage to which all the promises of God have been made. If he can only pay the price, then he is legally entitled to take and open the scroll.

John is then shown a mature, male lamb standing in front of the throne, and it has the appearance of having been killed. Of course it is symbolic of the sacrificial lambs of the Old Covenant that were one-year-old rams at the peak of maturity (Exodus 12:5). Quite plainly, this ram is none other than Jesus, and he has the necessary price for the redemption of the world. Revelation 5:9 reveals it: "*By thy blood thou didst ransom men for God from every tribe and tongue and people and nation.*" The price needed to cancel the demands of the righteous, holy God is the life-blood of a sinless son of man!

The blood of innocent Jesus, free of sin and shed on the cross at Calvary, was acceptable to God for the redeeming of the whole world. Hallelujah! What a simply wonderful moment! No wonder the multitudes in heaven break out into a crescendo of praise, thanksgiving, and worship of the Lamb and him who sits on the throne (Revelation 5:11–14).

When Jesus entered the innermost shrine of heaven, into the very presence of God the Father, he did so as our perfect High Priest, bearing his own blood (Hebrews 9:11–12). So the moments recorded here must have taken place following the ascension of Jesus into heaven to accomplish the very purpose of presenting his blood to his Father as full payment for the sin of the whole world.

Having received the scroll from his Father, Jesus began to open it (Revelation 5:7, 6:1). With the opening of the first seal, he sent the Holy Spirit into his world to begin the long process of bringing it back to God's order. How was this to be accomplished? Jesus was not going to rush in as he could have done, because he had a special work that he wanted to accomplish.

Now, all authority in heaven and on earth belongs to Jesus forever, but here on earth we do not yet see that dominion in place (Hebrews 2:8–9)—anything but! Jesus has a deliberate strategy by which to accomplish his purposes. His aim is not just to get followers for himself: he has a yet higher ambition in his heart. It is to have men and women who, through faithful obedience to "the truth" of the Word they have come to love, have completely rejected "the lie" from their lives and have become fit companions to rule with him in eternity. He calls them "conquerors" because under the New Covenant he has established with God, they exercise the power to overcome the iniquity in themselves, in the world around them and in Satan, the deceiver. *They truly are conquerors for Christ!*

In consequence of Jesus' victory and the opening of the first seal, Satan is muzzled and restrained. But by express permission from God, he still operates in the world so that disciples of Jesus can be perfected through his testing. They do not achieve a *public* victory, but a *hidden* victory of the heart, within the context of the life that King Jesus has prepared for each disciple he is training for glory.

This victory is only achievable at the cost of the shed blood of Jesus. It provides the only means by which the sins of men can be forgiven *and* their iniquity be completely destroyed. It is the blood that establishes a new covenant between God and those who accept it. It is not a blanket washing away of the sins of all men; rather it is the offering of a covenant by which those who accept its terms have their sins freely forgiven. But the covenant achieves more than a mere dealing with the past, wonderful though that is. Its terms require us to become disciples of Jesus, sons of God in training for glory.

In Isaiah 53:4–6 we read:

> *"Surely he has born our griefs (Hebrew: sicknesses) and carried our sorrows (Hebrew: pains); yet we esteemed him stricken, smitten by God and afflicted. But he was wounded for our transgressions, he was bruised for our iniquities; and upon him was the chastisement that made us whole, and with his stripes we are healed. All we like sheep have gone astray; we have turned each one to his own way; and the Lord has laid on him the iniquity of us all."*

The blood of Jesus has the power to wash away the sins of the past and it has the power to deal with the iniquity within our hearts. The indwelling presence of that power means that we need not sin anymore!

This is almost too much for most Christians to accept. Iniquity is so much a part of our lives (though we rarely dare to face it) that we find it impossible to believe we will ever be free of it! On the one hand, we claim to be "cleansed by the blood of the Lamb" while, on the other, we live to a standard of holiness that is virtually nonexistent! How has this come about?

All too often, an inadequate gospel of convenience is being preached and practised, even with signs and wonders, and it is deceptive. It is an "easy gospel" derived at the Tree of Knowledge of Good and Evil and proclaimed by unenlightened, religious men who have not themselves been set free. They strive to get a reputation and a following (plus a good living) while indulging the lusts of the flesh: those passions whose root is iniquity.

In many churches today, believers who do not know the Scriptures are encouraged to view themselves as sinners who will *always* go on sinning, as if this is inevitable. They are led in formal confession every time they assemble, as if there is no power available to help them break the endless cycle of sin and confession; they are forever stuck with their "human weaknesses" and resigned to have it so. Thus, doubting and uncertain, they excuse themselves from their responsibilities as sons of God to study the Word and lead their wives and families in the truth. They are not changed and so never grow up to spiritual maturity. This must certainly lead to backsliding sooner or later (See 2 Peter 2:20–22).

Hebrews is the great New Testament book that explains the power of the blood of the New Covenant to us. Consider what Hebrews 10:26–29, 36–39 says by way of warning on this subject:

> *"For if we sin deliberately (or wilfully) after receiving the (full) knowledge of the truth, there no longer remains a sacrifice for sin, but a fearful prospect of judgement, and a fury of fire which will consume the adversaries. A man who has violated the Law of Moses dies without mercy at the testimony of two or three witnesses. How much worse punishment do you think will be deserved by the man who has spurned the Son of God, and profaned the blood of the covenant by which he was sanctified, and outraged the Spirit of grace? . . . For you have need of endurance, so that you may do the will of God and receive what is promised. For yet a little while and the coming one shall come and shall not tarry; but my righteous one shall live by faith, and if he shrinks back, my soul has no pleasure in him'. But we are not of those who shrink back and are destroyed, but of those who have faith and keep their souls."*

A person becomes a Christian when he hears and receives the truth of the gospel. He is to understand that he is personally entering into the New Covenant with God just as the people of Israel understood and entered into *their* covenant with God. For them, its terms meant obeying a detailed code of behaviour *for life*. For us, there is a better deal: it is nothing less than an *exchange* of life! It is God's life in exchange for our life; Jesus' inheritance in glory for our destiny in hell; his character and nature for our corrupted soul and mind; and his righteousness for our iniquity. As we learn to put off the one by the obedience of faith, in order to put on the other, it is the end of sinning. God always calls for a whole life commitment. We may not opt in and out of his covenant. We must take our part very seriously. Jesus graphically called it, *"taking up our cross daily and following him"* . . . for as long as it takes.

THE CHURCH:
AN ARMY AND A FAMILY?

We are not left unaided to struggle against iniquity all by ourselves. Jesus had a wonderful plan for victory, which he initiated before he left this world. He had a two-part strategy for achieving this objective: individual and collective, personal and corporate.

Personal Discipleship

Any army is made up of many individuals, each trained to fight and defend himself. An army stands or falls upon the quality of the individual soldiers. Jesus told his disciples to enlist others who would in turn become disciples. One hymn writer called them "Soldiers of Christ."

Jesus told the Twelve:

> "*All authority in heaven and on earth has been given to me. Go therefore and make disciples of all nations, baptizing them in the name of the Father and of the Son and of the Holy Spirit, teaching them to observe all that I have commanded you; and lo, I am with you always even unto the close of the age*" (Matthew 28:18–20).

The Great Commission was the first part of Jesus' strategy for redemption. To fully understand his intention we need to observe both the context and the detail of these fundamental "marching orders"!

First, to return to the picture in Revelation 5, before he gives the Great Commission recorded in Matthew 28; it is clear that Jesus has received the scroll from Father's hand. He is Lord! His power is supreme. Satan is a defeated enemy. His "lie" has been exposed and "truth" is once more available to mankind. Truth to set them free to be what God always wanted them to be—his obedient children.

So now there is a four-part sequence to be followed. His first edict is to his disciples; it is an unequivocal command:

(1) "*Go and make disciples of all nations.*" The disciples understood from this that they were not making followers for themselves, but, as they themselves were, followers of Jesus. It is essential from the outset that every believer understands that he or she is to be a disciple of Jesus. This immediately frees us from any tendency to become focused on an individual spiritual leader, church, sect, or denomination rather than on Jesus. Such discipleship is initiated in baptism.

(2) *"Baptizing them in the name of the Father, and of the Son and of the Holy Spirit."* Believers who were convicted of sin and saw their need for salvation responded in heartfelt repentance.

The word "repentance" (In Hebrew, *shachah* and in Greek, *metanoien*) means "come to your senses and turn back." Those people who became disciples of Jesus did exactly that. It was the first step in being saved. They came to understand that the road they were on would lead to nowhere but hell and knew they must turn to God. They understood that by becoming Jesus' disciple, trusting in his death on their behalf, they would receive God's forgiveness and a new life that would be everlasting.

In order to be initiated into this new life, a symbolic act was required. This symbol of death and resurrection identified the new believer with Jesus' own death and resurrection, and is the Sacrament of Baptism.

Repentance includes an honest, personal assessment of one's true condition. Paul put it plainly in Romans 3:9–18:

> *". . . all men, both Jews and Greeks are under the power of iniquity, as it is written, 'None is righteous, no, not one; no one understands, no one seeks for God. All have turned aside, together they have gone wrong; no one does good, not even one. Their throat is an open grave, they use their tongues to deceive. The venom of asps is under their lips: their mouth is full of curses and bitterness. Their feet are swift to shed blood, in their paths are ruin and misery, and the way of peace they do not know. There is no fear of God before their eyes.'"*

Has Paul overstated his comments? Most of us are tempted to think that he must have done so. Surely things cannot be that bad!

We must never forget that God looks upon our hearts and so he is not deceived. We are being shown the results of hidden iniquity in the heart of man. We need to be convinced that the human heart (yes, ours too) cannot be cleaned up, that there is no cure for our iniquity—*it must be put to death.*

This is the message of the fall of both Satan and Adam—iniquity will inevitably separate man from God. Jesus ordains that baptism is the first step in the long process by which iniquity will be eradicated from the hearts of his disciples. Once baptism has taken place in the full name of the Triune God, Father, Son, and Holy Spirit, discipleship starts in earnest. The use of the triune name demonstrates that the full authority of God is committed to this step. Discipleship under Jesus the Lord begins here!

(3) *"Teaching them to observe all that I have commanded you."* The newly baptised is a new creature. Not by virtue of the *baptism itself,* for that is a symbol of death, but by virtue of being *resurrected to new life in Christ.* Rather as Noah and his family were saved *through* water because they were *in* the Ark! Peter speaks of this in his first letter (1 Peter 3:2b–22).

We cannot be a new creation before the old one has died. This is the mystery and true importance of baptism. Without faith in what it stands for, we cannot know ourselves to be a new creation and so we can never properly be a disciple. Jesus was careful to explain this important principle to Nicodemus (John 3:3–16).

As disciples, we each have a role to play in the growth and change of our brothers and sisters. They, in turn, have a role in *our* growth and development too. *We need each other* if Jesus is to accomplish his full purpose in us. *We need others*, in order to teach them to observe all that he has commanded *us* through his Word and by his Spirit. This speaks of interaction of life—a training process, in which we encourage and teach one another. This working out of life together is the process of sanctification. It is this that deals with our iniquity.

At this point, we must ask an awkward question. If church leaders are not true disciples themselves, how can they be sanctified or assist in the process of discipling others? Equally, without other disciples around us how shall we grow as disciples?

Heirs of the Reformation have always laid stress on "justification through grace by faith." They have been right to do so. But an over emphasis on this has sometimes led to an omission of a tough but vital element in justification, namely the *obedience of faith* leading to sanctification.

Justification, sanctification, and glorification are inseparable as elements of our salvation. Justification rests upon the basis of what Jesus did for us. Sanctification rests upon the same basis but requires our deliberate daily participation in the process of change from the "old man" to the "new man." Glorification is what Jesus has already done for us, but which we will receive only when we have completed the course. It is not possible to separate them from each other and there is danger when we try to do so.

There are many Christians in the world today. There are many more church attenders. The great question is, how many *disciples* are there? How many Christians today accept the discipline and accountability needed to be a disciple? Without true discipleship, we have missed the first part of the kingdom strategy that Jesus established to bring us to glory with him. Without discipleship, there can be no sanctification. Without sanctification, there can be no inner change. Without inner change, our iniquity is not being dealt with. We have no personal testimony as to the effect that Christ has in our lives and no ministry to others. Without inner change, there is no growth to spiritual maturity and we will not be ready at Jesus' coming.

The devil is desperate to keep his control of people even after they have been saved. He can only do this when we allow him to blind us to the truth revealed by the Holy Spirit. For the Spirit of God seeks to show us our iniquity and attendant sins on a daily basis, not to depress us but to show us there is a way out if only we will face them fairly and squarely and act accordingly.

(4) *"And lo I am with you always, even unto the end of the age."* It has been said, "A text removed from its context becomes a pretext." This wonderful promise is just such a case. It must not be made to stand in isolation. The "and" links the promise to what has been said before. The promise of Jesus' presence with us is conditional upon our fulfilling the commands that precede it. In other words, if we are not disciples, doing the work of discipling others, Jesus will not be with us!

The presence of Jesus in his church depends upon his church following his strategy. If we adopt some other strategy, or decide to neglect a part of Jesus' total strategy, how then can he fulfil *his* part? If Jesus is not head of his church how then can the church be *his* body? How many of us even know that we should actually have Jesus' presence within us day by day, moment by moment? Sadly, in so many cases, he simply cannot be there.

In his first letter, John wrote:

> *"This is the message we have heard from him and proclaim to you, that God is light and in him is no darkness at all. If we say we have fellowship with him while we walk in darkness, we lie and do not live according to the truth; but if we walk in the light as he is in the light, we have fellowship with one another, and the blood of Jesus cleanses us from all iniquity. If we say we have no iniquity, we deceive ourselves and the truth is not in us. If we confess our sins, he is faithful and just and will forgive us our sins and cleanse us from all iniquity. If we say we have not sinned we make him a liar"* (1 John 1:5–10).

We should always remember that conviction of sin is not condemnation. We should always remember that sins emanate from iniquity in the heart. We need both our sins forgiven and our iniquity put to death, in order that we may stand in our status as sons of God.

Corporate Relationship

The second part of Jesus' strategy is his family—the sons of God—living together in harmony.

The word "disciple" occurs many times in the gospel accounts and in Acts, but after that the word does not occur again. Had things changed by the time the epistles were written? Well, perhaps yes, because Jesus had changed them at the last moment. Just before his death Jesus prayed a heart-rending prayer to his Father and John recorded it in John 17. This prayer changed everything. It was both revelation and prophecy. It related to an eternal objective and it uniquely pointed to the nature of the true church for which Jesus will return as a bridegroom for a bride.

Jesus was praying for a unity amongst his disciples that would be equal to the unity existing in God himself. It was this prayer that defined the second part of Jesus' strategy to reclaim his kingdom. The church was to be a fellowship of his disciples—his family here on earth. The main title given to believers in the epistles is "brethren." The Lord's disciples had become his brothers and consequently brothers of each other. There is no gender involved in this any more than when we speak of all (both male and female) being "sons of God." These terms speak of a *spiritual* relationship that claims the whole being of each disciple.

The basis of this humanly impossible relationship is that Jesus is in each one. A presence that, as we have already seen, is dependent upon the believer's walk of discipleship. The original, unique oneness of Adam and Eve is to be witnessed by the world in the family of God. But, for all the intimacy of family relationship, the conditions of discipleship are not thereby relaxed. Rather they are reinforced!

These two elements of Jesus' strategy—the personal and the corporate—are interdependent and that surely is not surprising, for Jesus wants us to have the character and nature of our heavenly Father. As human children, we bear the stamp of our forebears; now, as born-again sons of God, we are to bear the stamp of our divine Father. He is light and love—that is how we are to be. Everything that he is, we are to be. For this magnificent purpose to be achieved, we must be changed and continue in the process of change (sanctification). None can accomplish this alone. We need each other desperately.

There is so much to be taught concerning these things, but for now the issue is this: do you agree with this proposition or do you not? Do you believe that it is necessary for you to be a *disciple* in order to defeat Satan? Do you believe that you need your brothers and sisters, not just as other members of the same congregation, but also as living members of one another, the Body of Christ, the true church of which Jesus is the head? A fellowship of people ready to face reality and live in it, who need to learn to love you, just as they need you to love them?

It is easy to answer yes to these questions because they make things sound so good, but be warned, there is a cost involved, which many are not prepared to face up to. We shall discover more of this as we go on.

I'll let Paul provide the final charge to this chapter:

"I therefore, a prisoner for the Lord, beg you to lead a life worthy of the calling to which you have been called, with all lowliness and meekness, with patience, forbearing one another in love, eager to maintain the unity

of the Spirit in the bond of peace. There is one body and one Spirit, just as you were called to the one hope that belongs to your call, one Lord, one faith, one baptism, one God and Father of us all, who is above all and through all and in all. But grace was given to each of us according to the measure of Christ's gift. Therefore it is said, "When he ascended on high he led a host of captives, and he gave gifts to men." (In saying, "He ascended," what does it mean but that he also descended into the lower parts of the earth? He who descended is also he who ascended far above all the heavens, that he might fill all things.) And his gifts were that some should be apostles, some prophets, some evangelists, some pastors and teachers, to equip the saints for the work of ministry, for building up the body of Christ, until we attain to the unity of the faith and of the knowledge of the son of God, to mature manhood, to the measure of the stature of the fullness of Christ; so that we may be no longer children tossed to and fro and carried about by every wind of doctrine, by the cunning of men, by their craftiness in deceitful wiles. Rather, speaking the truth in love, we are to grow up in every way into him who is the head, into Christ, from whom the whole body, joined and knit together in every joint with which it is supplied, when each part is working properly, makes bodily growth and upbuilds itself in love" (Ephesians 4:1–16).

THE APOSTATE CHURCH:
IS IT US OR THEM?

Prophecies in the New Testament concerning the "end times," point to the existence of a church that has lost its way completely.

Are we there now? Are *we* the apostate church of the end times? Are we the church given over to deceitful spirits and doctrines of demons (1 Timothy 4:1)? Are *we* supporting the church that has a form of religion but denies the power of it (2 Timothy 3:5)? We have to face these searching questions.

Such is the nature of church disunity that we will be tempted to apply these prophetic Scripture verses to every church other than our own! But the truth is that the fault exposed by these prophecies is so fundamental that all without exception are involved. We are all deceived by the deceiver and the deception is the same as it ever was! Iniquity in the heart!

Iniquity is a deeply rooted corruption every bit as unholy, stinking, dark, and unchallenged as it was in Adam's time. Paul describes it as "the mystery of iniquity" (2 Thessalonians 2:7). He knew even then that it would trouble the church through the ages continually.

Iniquity is a mystery because it is hidden from sight within the hearts of men and women. Only through the sins we actually commit does its presence become apparent, but unless that root in the heart is identified and understood it can never be dealt with in an appropriate and effective way. Sins can be confessed and forgiven, but the hidden root remains undisturbed, shrouded in mystery, because it cannot be seen.

Everywhere we look in the churches we find greed, immorality, struggles for power, hatred, and selfishness both at the grass roots and at leadership levels, often publicly expressed and without shame. This level of indulgence and tolerance of private, immoral practices that are never accepted in Scripture, is but the latest and most scary stage of a long slide. The issues are so overwhelming that we scarcely know where to start in addressing them.

It all stems from that deeper, underlying problem that is as old as this world. No matter whether immoral thoughts, words, and deeds are prompted by the devil or the flesh, they all take root in the human heart, and from there iniquity pours out as sin in its various forms. If we refuse to recognise it, we are powerless to bring the correction ordained by God in his Word. Where there is toleration of iniquity its demands will only increase. Through not accepting God's Word as providing the divine basis for our deliverance from sins and iniquity, we are as powerless to resist as Adam and Eve were in the beginning at the Tree of Knowledge of Good and Evil. The consequences now are as dreadful as they were then. Once we move away from God's

Word and the insight given us by the Holy Spirit we are adrift in the restless sea of spin, propaganda, and politics. By these means, Satan rules through fallen mankind, even in the church.

Human behaviour has never changed because the heart of man has never changed. In the foolishness and fond imaginings of evolutionary theories, we like to think that we are improving as a race. Hard evidence shows that while culture, economics, and laws may modify public behaviour, the inner man is without control of himself because he remains a son of fallen Adam. Statistical analysis of all kinds shows that today's church members cheat, fornicate, lie, and fight just like the world. Helpful and cautionary though such analysis might be, it can only tell us that the church is failing; it cannot tell us how to change the situation. Only the Scriptures can do that. "*Be sure of this, that no fornicator or impure man, or one who is covetous (that is an idolater), has any inheritance in the kingdom of Christ and of God.* **Let no one deceive you with empty words***, for it is because of these things that the wrath of God comes upon the sons of disobedience*" (Ephesians 5:5–6).

Empty words produce deception, and deception is everywhere. Indulgent teaching undermines the absolutes of Scripture, providing an imagined set of excuses for all manner of wickedness.

We are in a desperate condition. We have become just like the people of Israel in their time. We are fat, lazy, complacent, unrighteous, and idolatrous, far more intent upon our own comforts and pleasures than the things of Almighty God. As sons of disobedience, we are deceived by our own hearts to believe that our self-centred, self-indulgent lives represent the salvation that Jesus so painfully made available to us. The contrast between "the truth" and "the lie" is so enormous that it might be comical if it were not so desperately tragic. Indeed it provides the enemies of Christ with a constant supply of material enabling them to demean and ridicule both our faith and our Saviour.

In 1 Timothy 4:1–3, Paul warns his young friend:

"*Now the Spirit expressly says that in later times some will depart from the faith by giving heed to* **deceitful** *spirits and doctrines of demons, through the pretensions of liars whose consciences are seared, who forbid marriage and enjoin abstinence from foods which God created to be received with thanksgiving by those who believe and know the truth.*"

Then again, in 2 Timothy 3:1–5, Paul goes on:

"*But understand this, that in the last days there will come times of stress. For men will be lovers of self, lovers of money, proud, arrogant, abusive, disobedient to their parents, ungrateful, unholy, inhuman, implacable, slanderers, profligates, fierce, haters of good, treacherous, reckless, swollen with conceit, lovers of pleasure rather than lovers of God, holding the form of religion but denying the power of it. Avoid such people.*" Clearly Paul is not describing society at large. This is the church!

Peter adds to the exposure when he writes in 2 Peter 3:3–14:

"*First of all you must understand this, that scoffers will come in the last days with scoffing, following their own passions and saying, 'Where is the promise of his coming? For ever since the fathers fell asleep, all things have continued as they were from the beginning of creation'. They deliberately ignore this fact, that by the word of God heavens existed long ago, and an earth formed out of water and by means of water, through which the world that then existed was deluged with water and perished. But by the same word the heavens and earth that now exist have been stored up for fire, being kept until the day of judgment and destruction of ungodly men…Since all these things are thus to be dissolved, what sort of persons ought you to be in lives of holiness and godliness, waiting for and hastening the coming of the day of God, because of which the heavens will be kindled and dissolved, and the elements will melt with fire! But according to his promise we wait for new heavens and a new earth in which righteousness dwells. Therefore, beloved, since you wait for these, be zealous to be found by him without spot or blemish, and at peace."*

Then again in Jude 1: 17–23 we have further revelation concerning these days:

"But you must remember, beloved, the predictions of the apostles of our Lord Jesus Christ; they said to you, 'In the last times there will be scoffers, following their own ungodly passions'. It is these people who set up divisions, worldly people, devoid of the Spirit. But you, beloved, build yourselves up on your most holy faith; pray in the Holy Spirit; keep yourselves in the love of God; wait for the mercy of our Lord Jesus Christ unto eternal life. And convince some, who doubt; save some, by snatching them out of the fire; on some have mercy with fear, hating even the garment spotted by the flesh."

According to the prophetic outline by the apostles, the appalling conditions in the church in the end times will not be confined to a particular area of the world or any particular denomination; it will be worldwide. It is not a minor matter but so major that it touches everyone and everything in the church's life. Viewed from God's perspective, the outcome can only be disastrous. Indeed, Jesus made a particularly alarming remark in regard to this when he said, *". . . when the Son of Man comes, will he find faith in the earth?"* (Luke 18:8). The implication is devastating.

Churches may be able to point to thousands of adherents, to magnificent buildings, to outreach programmes, and good works of every kind, but if they are not dealing with iniquity in the hearts of men they are simply providing a wide gate and an easy way that Jesus said would lead to destruction (Matthew 7:13–14).

Far from being ready for the time of his coming, such is our prosperous complacency, that instead of joyful anticipation, there is only ignorance and apathy. "One will be taken and one left," Jesus said of that day. The question is, why is one left behind? To those in the churches who are still living by the fruit of the Tree of Knowledge, warnings of divine judgment and punishment are to be treated with disdain and even contempt.

The problem of iniquity has been with us ever since Adam and Eve left the Garden of Eden. It is the problem that caused Cain to kill Abel and that led directly to the state of man's heart defined by God in Genesis 6:5 and 8:21. It is the problem that constantly afflicted the Israelites and ultimately defeated them. It is the problem that under Satan's heavy hand is defeating the formal church today. The deception is so all encompassing and effective that we can hardly see where the true church is. We are indeed in dire straits.

"THIS GOSPEL SHALL BE PREACHED THROUGHOUT THE WORLD AND THEN THE END WILL COME"

We should not be surprised at what we see around us today, for Jesus took care to forewarn us in specific terms. To be forewarned is to be forearmed. But if we are to be forearmed, we must know, believe, and understand those warnings. Recorded in Matthew chapters 24 and 25 is detailed teaching Jesus gave his disciples concerning the last days.

Although like other biblical prophecies covering this period of time, there are problems of interpretation needing to be faced, the central truths of the teaching are clear. In order to receive maximum understanding of these chapters, we need a wide knowledge of prophetic teaching and insight given by the Holy Spirit in the rest of the Bible. As Peter warns us: *"First of all you must understand this, that no prophecy of scripture is a matter of one's own interpretation, because no prophecy ever came by the impulse of man, but men moved by the Holy Spirit spoke from God"* (2 Peter 1:20–21).

The prophetic statements in the Bible are given primarily for the purpose of warning God's people of what is to come so that they can prepare themselves. Thus there is an element of foretelling future events, but this is accompanied by what God is saying to his people for *immediate* action! For example, John the Baptiser came saying prophetically, *"Repent, for the kingdom of heaven is at hand!"* (Matthew 3:2). He was calling the people to repentance because of the soon appearance of Messiah.

In Matthew 24:2, Jesus prophesied concerning the great Temple in Jerusalem, *"You see all these, do you not? Truly I say to you, there will not be left here one stone upon another that will not be thrown down."*

These words provoked a response from the disciples just as any authentic prophecy would raise questions with all of us. They recognised that such events would affect them and they wanted to be in a position to respond appropriately.

Jesus' teaching on this subject was not public. He was teaching his disciples privately because only they would have the faith to handle what they were hearing. This remains true today! Only Jesus' disciples, who are looking for his coming, will have the faith to search for the truth behind the prophecies. For the world at large, such topics are a matter for scorn.

The major problem in the churches is that interpretation of Bible prophecy is considered to be so contentious that it is unreliable and even unhelpful to attempt it. Anything that speaks of Jesus' soon return or of the end of the world meets with special scorn. But 80 percent of all biblical prophecy has already been fulfilled and the accuracy of those prophecies has been proven by history. The same record, however, demonstrates how the people for whom the prophecies were intended generally failed to benefit from them either through ignorance or unbelief. How tragic! How vital it is for modern disciples to get understanding of the last 20 percent that has yet to be fulfilled!

The disciples wanted to know three things from Jesus (Matthew 24:3):

1. When would the Temple be destroyed?
2. When would Jesus come?
3. When would the end of the world come?

Jesus replied with a remarkable, in depth teaching recorded in Matthew 24 and 25. Jesus' answers to those questions span an enormous time gap. Thus, the forthcoming destruction of Herod's Temple in AD 70 merges with references to the Lord's Second Coming as if they were a combined event with no intervening years. As it is, nearly 2000 years have passed since Titus laid siege to Jerusalem and we still await the return of the Lord.

It is as if Jesus wrote the three answers to the questions onto separate transparencies and projected them together on a screen as one picture. The result is an intermingling of information that needs to be separated into its constituent parts by discernment and by comparison with other prophecy on the subjects covered. The disciples must have been completely baffled by his teaching at the time they heard it. Much would be clarified for them once Jesus had been crucified and raised from the dead. Over the following forty years, they would see his predictions unfolding before their eyes and they would understand what was taking place.

Jesus chose his words carefully because they would need to speak with divine, prophetic clarity to *every* generation of disciples that would follow, and especially that generation living through the last days—*our* generation! The graphic warnings of Jesus were given to prepare his disciples to stand against deception and to prepare for persecution: his warnings would need to be understood and accepted in order that end-time disciples would not be led astray.

As we embark on an exploration of Matthew 24 and 25, we note that Jesus first deals with those events that the disciples themselves might live to see. It would be a time of great violence and upheaval. The whole nation would be increasingly politically, economically, and socially unsettled, chafing, along with the nations round about, against the yoke of imperialist Rome. This would also be a time of religious chaos when false messiahs would arise seeking to deceive the people. *"But,"* Jesus says in Matthew 24:6, *"the end is not yet."*

The fall of Jerusalem would initiate an upsurge of strife between nations and civil war within them. A series of natural disasters would lead to widespread famine, but on a localised level. These signs would be repeated in a much later generation, but on a worldwide scale. In Matthew 24:8, Jesus says, *"This is but the* **beginning** *of the birth pangs."* In other words, things are beginning to happen but there are worse pains to come.

Jesus then carefully spells out the signs that will immediately precede his coming, and we need to know what they are.

- *They will deliver you up to tribulation, and put you to death;*
- *You will be hated by all nations for my name's sake.*
- *Many will fall away, betray one another, and hate one another.*
- *Many false prophets will arise and lead many astray.*
- *Because wickedness (iniquity) is multiplied*

- *Most men's love will grow cold.*
- *He who endures to the end will be saved.*
- *This gospel of the kingdom will be preached throughout the whole world as a testimony to all nations;*
- *Then the end will come* (Matthew 24:9–14).

In this awesome passage, Jesus is warning his disciples—his faithful church—that a great faith-test will come in the last days. This will be a time of tribulation when his disciples will once again suffer acute persecution prior to the coming of Jesus for his church—his bride.

Multitudes of Jesus' disciples have been through such testing in the past, and in dying they have passed into Paradise. Of course, not all disciples are called to die a martyr's death. But all are tested, and having become conquerors, they too wait in Paradise for that great day of the Lord when he comes for them. They endured suffering knowing the promise that they will be raised in their incorruptible bodies at the moment when Jesus comes and will be snatched up with the faithful believers who are still alive at that time. All will receive their glorious, incorruptible, resurrection bodies in that moment and go up to their Father's house, following Jesus into heaven for the marriage supper of the Lamb.

But let us be clear that for those disciples who are alive in the period immediately before the return of Jesus for his bride, life will be very hard. Jesus deliberately chooses the word "tribulation" to describe this time of trial. Some will be imprisoned, even suffering a martyr's death, having been betrayed by those who they have loved and worked with in the church. Genuine disciples will remain faithful to *the truth*.

Just as Jesus was betrayed by one of his closest friends and was then put to death by a conspiracy between the spiritual and secular authorities, so may we be. It is our brothers and sisters and leaders in the churches who will betray us under pressure from the world (just as what happened in Rwanda in 1994). Jesus gave the reason for this in Matthew 24:12. He said, "*Because wickedness (iniquity) is multiplied*" these things would happen. This is not the world he is talking about, but the church. Iniquity will multiply in the church!

In 2 Thessalonians 2:9–12, Paul wrote of these same future events:

> "*The coming of the lawless one (or 'man of iniquity') by the activity of Satan will be with all power and with pretended signs and wonders, and with all wicked deception (lit: 'deceit of iniquity') for those who are to perish, because they refused to love the truth and so be saved. Therefore God sends upon them a strong delusion to make them believe what is false ('the lie') so that all may be condemned who did not believe the truth but had pleasure in unrighteousness (or 'iniquity').*"

The nature of the testing of the disciples is clear. They are required to stand in the truth of Scripture at a time when virtually the whole church will be against them, having been led astray in apostasy by believing "the lie." The specific nature of this apostasy (as we have seen above) is that sanctification is no longer understood, practised, or taught in the church at large. The church has a form of religion but denies the power of it.

[The word "wicked" used in 2:10 is one of a number of English words, like sin, lawlessness, rebellion, or unrighteousness that are used by modern translators to render two Greek words into English. These words, *adikia* and *anomia*, equate with the common Old Testament Hebrew words for iniquity (a word no longer ordinarily used in English). Translating these words in this way is not wrong, but it loses the continuity of the special significance that the word iniquity carries as being the particular word for the problem of the heart that first afflicted mankind in Eden. Without this word, the issue becomes fogged by the use of other less specific words. Perhaps this is no accident after all; *adikia* means literally "without righteousness" and *anomia* means "without law,"—both accurately describe iniquity but do not encompass its whole meaning.]

First John 3:4 has this to teach us: *"Everyone who commits sin (armartia) is guilty of lawlessness (anomia); sin is lawlessness (anomia)";* thus he links together the heart condition of lawlessness (or iniquity) with sins—the things we do that impact our surroundings. Sin is to be distinguished from sins. By using the word iniquity for that original sin, we avoid the difficulties encountered when we use other English words that are not reflected in the Hebrew or Greek. Thus in 1 John 1:7–10, a literal rendering gives the following:

> *"But if we walk in the light as he is in the light, we have fellowship with one another and the blood of Jesus cleanses us from all iniquity. If we say we have no iniquity, we deceive ourselves and the truth is not in us. If we confess our sins, he is faithful and just to forgive us our sins and cleanse us from all iniquity. If we say we have not sinned we make him a liar and the truth is not in us".*

This is followed by some startling statements:

> *"Little children, let no one deceive you. He who does right is righteous, as he is righteous. He who commits sin (amartia—sins) is of the devil; for the devil has sinned (amartano—committed sins) from the beginning . . . No one born of God commits sin (amartia); for God's nature (seed) abides in him, and he cannot sin (amartano—commit sins) because he is born of God. By this it may be seen who are the children of God, and who are the children of the devil: whoever does not do right is not of God, nor he who does not love his brother"* (1 John 3:7–10).

To make sense of this and accord with other parts of Scripture, it is necessary to see that John is not talking here about lapses into disobedience that we all have from time to time and of which we must confess and repent, but about known, ongoing sins, which we are tempted to indulge and continue in while still claiming to be God's children.

These are often familiar to us from habit. Ways of thinking, speaking, doing, and even feeling, which we excuse in ourselves, being deceived by our own heart. How many are trapped by just such deception—often in the name of "love"? Since all sins arise out of iniquity in the heart, we are indulging iniquity when we go on sinning. This allows the power of iniquity to grow. Thus, we function like children of Satan.

Jesus then says to his disciples in Matthew 24:12 that a mark of the church at the end will be an increase in iniquity, which will lead to the love of most growing cold, the very opposite of the true church. Those who continue to witness to the truth by their lives will become an increasing embarrassment to the church at large and become objects of hate as far as the world is concerned. This is when the betrayals will take place as so-called "Christians" who have fallen away seek to save their own skins.

The church worldwide has already reached a state when unacknowledged iniquity is rapidly and visibly increasing. Many orthodox Bible doctrines that have sustained believers for two thousand years have been abandoned. Having substituted their own doctrines in place of Christ's, most churches are powerless to confront the sin and iniquity in their ranks. Already the "love" of multitudes of church attenders is merely outward religious form and lip service. Because of this sweeping deception, many of those who claim to be children of God are living their lives as children of the devil. Unless the true gospel of the kingdom is preached to them, they have no one and nothing to help them.

This gospel (Matthew 24:14) is the one that Jesus said must be preached throughout the whole world before the end. This is the Watchman's work:

- To preach the gospel of faith in the whole Word of God: leading to salvation; leading to discipleship; leading to daily sanctification and change; leading to warning others as a Watchman for Jesus; leading to victory as a conqueror; leading to glory at the coming of Jesus.
- To preach the gospel that calls for the endurance of believers in the face of a great final testing of their faith.
- To preach the gospel that refuses to tolerate iniquity and sin at a time of apostasy and compromise in the churches.
- To preach the gospel that may result in those who preach it being ostracized, rejected, betrayed, and even killed by those they have loved and with whom they have served—as it was for Jesus!

Anything less than this is "another gospel" and is deception.

Things will be bad in the earth for faithful disciples as they pass through the tribulation of those times. But after the rapture of the saints, matters will get substantially worse. Then begins the "last week" of Daniel's great prophecy concerning Israel. During this period of seven years, God brings matters to a dreadful, fearful conclusion. First comes the *Great* Tribulation. Orchestrated by God's angels, it will overtake the whole world during the first three-and-a-half-year period when the church has gone from the earth to be with her beloved bridegroom, Jesus, in his Father's house. The Antichrist world ruler will prove to be powerless to control affairs and will seek to vent his wrath on the Jews.

After this, the righteous, pent up wrath of God will be unleashed upon the remaining multitudes of angry, bitter, and resentful people on earth. In their rebellion, they will have consistently refused every warning. Even in the face of God's judgements, they will refuse to repent, choosing rather to curse God. Their iniquity will be full and the earth will reap the terrible harvest.

INIQUITY IN THE OLD TESTAMENT

The Hebrew word translated as "iniquity" occurs about 250 times in the Old Testament, making its use more frequent than the word for "sin" with which it is interchangeable, and with which we are more familiar. However, because its meaning is little understood, the word has all but disappeared from modern translations, being replaced by less accurate alternatives. But this can cause problems, for while these are not necessarily wrong, no alternative catches the full sense of the original English word iniquity.

We have seen already that iniquity is the spiritual disease that, passed on to us all from Adam, separates us from our Creator God. If we are to fully comprehend the iniquity-problem with which we all have to grapple daily, both within ourselves and in others around us, then a study of its origins and its history is a necessity. As one of the principles of biblical interpretation (hermeneutics) is the principle of "first mention", the first use of the word in the Bible is a good place to begin our study.

This occurs in Genesis 15, a chapter in which God confirms by solemn covenant the wonderful promise he had previously made to a childless Abram. In verse 6, bearing in mind that Abram had iniquity in his heart just as we all do, we read an amazing statement. God told Abram that his descendants would be as numerous as the stars in the heavens, and *Abram believed the Lord; and he reckoned it to him as righteousness.* (Genesis 15:6)

Right here, God establishes the principle that a man or woman's faith in his Word is the basis of him or her being accepted by God as righteousness. Thus faith in God's Word is the prerequisite for our dealing with our iniquity. Speaking of the power of the gospel, Paul writes, "For *in it the righteousness of God is revealed through faith for faith; as it is written, "He who through faith is righteous shall live ."*" It would remain true under every dispensation of God's dealings with mankind and in all generations, and it is in this sense that all who have faith in God's Word become "sons of Abraham".

It seems that God had brought Abram and his family out of Ur into the land of the Chaldeans in order that he might give them ownership of that land. But here we are presented with a great mystery because this land of promise was already occupied by many tribes when Abram got there; how could one man and his small family take possession of it? God showed Abram (later becoming Abraham), that he would not personally inherit the land, but his heirs would. God would not only bring Abraham's family into the land, but he would use them to bring his judgement on the tribes who were in possession of the land, and upon the great nation of Egypt (unnamed here) who would hold them in slavery for a very long time. In a few remarkable sentences God foretells the future of the lands of the Middle East four hundred years before it would happen, and the reason why.

The critical insight into this plan of God is found in the single sentence, *"for the iniquity of the Amorites is not yet complete."* (Genesis 15:16b) 400 long years would pass before this irredeemable condition would be reached by these people. Of the ten nations that occupied the land promised to Abram, the Amorites were the most corrupted and tolerant of wickedness. Their behaviour, was particularly extreme. This display of iniquity, shared by all ten nations, would burgeon and grow over the years until God would be forced to eliminate it by the total destruction of them all, and the yet future nation of Israel would be the instrument by which he would execute his judgement on them. Because God does not change, this story is prophetic of the future of the whole world: *where iniquity is not dealt with by the people themselves responding to God's revealed order, inevitably it will grow worse and worse until God himself must destroy those people.* In the supposedly sophisticated world we occupy today many types of ancient Egypt and many tribes like those Amorites of old can be found. Their end will be no different.

To fully comprehend what was taking place and to identify the source of the problem God was revealing, we must take further steps back in time. Who were these tribes occupying the land God was giving to Abram? How come they were they so much more wicked than other nations around them so that God would have to make an example of them, and mete out ruthless judgement upon them? Back in Genesis 10:6, we read that the sons of Ham were Cush, Egypt, Put and Canaan (the youngest) and it was these particular tribes who, after the Flood, had settled in Canaan and in the other lands that we know today as the Middle East.

Ham was Noah's middle son (see Genesis 6:10). In the Bible he is distinguished by his inappropriate behaviour when he found his father drunkenly exposed in his tent (Genesis 9:20). (To us this curious behaviour seems to be of little significance, but the patriarchal culture of the time was very clear. Recognising the nature of iniquity, it made any disrespect of a "father" by a son (or other family member) a very serious offence. In this case it revealed an unacceptably rebellious and light hearted disposition in the son). Noah's resultant curse on him, prophesied what the future consequences of this act of gross disrespect would be as Ham's iniquity was passed down to his heirs: their errant and insincere behaviour would lead them to become servants to their brother tribes.

Going back further still in time, even before these events, the Bible shows us the effects of iniquity in some of the unclean spirits who were on the earth. In Genesis 6:1–4, there is an account of a horrific rebellion of fallen angels. They coupled with humans to produce mutant giants as their offspring. This was in all likelihood a consequence of extreme occult and deviant practices on the part of human beings, and the Bible provides no details of the revolting events that led to it, but it was clearly a satanic attempt to corrupt the bloodline of man through which would come the promised one who would "bruise Satan's head" (Genesis 3:15).

The iniquity that had passed from Satan into Adam at the Fall continued to express itself throughout that primeval time and we are provided with God's own view of the situation:

> *"The Lord saw that the wickedness of man was great in the earth and that every imagination of the thoughts of his heart was only evil continually. And the Lord was sorry he had made man on the earth, and it grieved him to his heart"* (Genesis 6:5–6). And: *"Now the earth was corrupt in God's sight and filled with violence. And God saw that the earth was corrupt, and behold, it was corrupt for all flesh had corrupted their way upon the earth. And God said to Noah, 'I have determined to make an end of all flesh; for the earth is filled with violence through them; behold I will destroy them with the earth'"* (Genesis 6:11–13).

Noah found favour with God because he was a righteous man by faith (the only one left on the earth), and God determined to use him to restart the whole process of his plan of salvation. But there was a problem. In spite of his personal and remarkable faith, Noah inevitably had iniquity in him and had passed it on to his family. God, the supreme realist, acknowledged this fact after the Flood: *"I will never again curse the ground because of man, for the imagination of man's heart is evil from his youth (so this must include Noah); neither will I ever again destroy every living creature as I have done. While the earth remains, seedtime and harvest, cold and heat, summer and winter, day and night shall not cease*" (Genesis 8:21–22).

God has been faithful to that promise for thousands of years despite man's best endeavours to provoke him. He knew that the Flood could not deal with the problem of iniquity. He knew full well that men would very soon disregard the double warning presented by the curse recorded in Genesis 3:17–19 and by the Flood, and would even come to treat the glorious rainbow in the sky as just another accidental atmospheric phenomenon! But those warnings were there for those who had eyes to see and ears to hear. They still are.

In Abraham's day, some three hundred years after the Flood, the situation in the Promised Land had again deteriorated so far that we find the second use of the word iniquity. It is used by the angels who came to save Lot and his family from the judgement pronounced upon Sodom and Gomorrah. According to Genesis 19:15 (KJV) the wickedness of the people living in those cities merited use of the word iniquity to describe it, and it incurred God's awful judgement. The particular expression of iniquity in those notorious Cities of the Plain was endemic practice of homosexuality (a clear indication to us that the source of all sexual immorality resides within the human heart).

After 400 years of slavery in Egypt, nothing had changed in the behaviour of the nations. Terrible immorality and the grossest forms of idolatry were common place. When God was preparing Moses to undertake his monumental work of welding a rabble of Hebrew slaves into the ordered nation of Israel, he took the unprecedented step of personally telling Moses his name—a privilege almost beyond belief .

> "*And the Lord descended in the cloud and stood with him there, and proclaimed the name of the Lord. The Lord passed before him, and proclaimed, 'The Lord, the Lord, a God merciful and gracious, slow to anger and abounding in steadfast love and faithfulness, keeping steadfast love for thousands, forgiving iniquity, transgression and sin, but who will by no means clear the guilty, visiting the iniquity of the fathers upon the children and the children's children to the third and fourth generation.' And Moses made haste to bow his face to the earth, and worshipped*" (Exodus 34:5–8).

Just like Adam, all men have passed on their iniquity to their children. The corruption inherited by Cain (and Abel) became the experience of all. All would have to fight that same inner beast that desired to overwhelm Cain, but the promise made to Cain would also prove true: "*If you do well will you not be accepted?*" God wants to pardon us. He longs to forgive us, but without our own desire and determination to take advantage of his offers, iniquity is still lodged in the heart, and God can do nothing for us.

In his next great step of mercy, the Lord God gave the Law to Abram's heirs through Moses. Provision was made for an annual act of atonement for the iniquity that was in them and acceptable sacrifices they must offer for their inevitable sins. The keeping of the Law would enable God to bless them materially and would make them invincible in the face of their enemies. But disobeying the Law and its terms would bring cursing in place of blessing.

Israel had an awesome job to do. "*Now therefore, if you will obey my voice and keep my covenant, you shall be my own possession among all the peoples; for the earth is mine, and you shall be to me a kingdom of priests and a holy nation*" (Exodus 19:5–6). Part of this task was to execute God's righteous judgement on the nations around them.

Israel's destiny was to make God, his holiness, judgement and mercy, known in the earth once again. Their ability to fulfil that destiny would be dependent upon their faith-obedience to the Covenant of Law. The first phase of that destiny was an invasion of Canaan—entry into the Promised Land, to cleanse it and bring it into God's order. Many Christians, not knowing the Scriptures and not understanding that man with iniquity in his heart is totally incorrigible and rebellious against God, wonder how a loving God could instruct his chosen people to slaughter others. By any standard it was a terrible sequence of death, but it demonstrated the seriousness of iniquity and the sins that are its expression. These nations were incorrigible, and their judgement provided a lesson both for Israel as well as for the Gentile nations, and even for us who would come later. *The stark truth is that God will by no means forgive the guilty.* If Israel were to fail in its appointed task of ridding the land of these tribes with their hideous practices, then it was only a matter of time before they themselves would be corrupted by their tolerance of them, and this would make it impossible for the nation to fulfil its God-given role in the world.

The heathen tribes in the Promised Land stand symbolically for the grip of iniquity on the hearts and lives of all men, blocking God from his desire to bless them. As a result they were dominated by demons; they worshipped idols, even offering their children as sacrifices by burning them alive in the fires on the altars.

Today, it seems that we are largely ignorant of these obscure but very relevant passages of the Bible:

"Behold, I make a covenant. Before all your people I will do marvels, such as have not been wrought in all the earth or in any nation; and all the people among whom you are shall see the work of the Lord; for it is a terrible thing I will do with you. Observe what I command you this day. Behold I will drive out the Amorites . . .Take heed to yourself, lest you make a covenant with the inhabitants of the land whither you go, lest it become a snare in the midst of you. You shall tear down their altars, and break their pillars, and cut down their Asherim (for you shall worship no other god, for the Lord whose name is Jealous, is a jealous God), lest you make a covenant with the inhabitants of the land, and when they play the harlot after their gods and sacrifice to their gods and one invites you, you eat of his sacrifice and you take their daughters for your sons, and their daughters play the harlot after their gods and make your sons play the harlot after their gods" (Exodus 34:10–16).

"When you come into the land which the Lord your God gives you, you shall not learn to follow the abominable practices of those nations. There shall not be found among you anyone who burns his son or his daughter as an offering, anyone who practices divination, a soothsayer, or an augur, or a sorcerer, or a charmer, or a medium, or a wizard, or a necromancer. For whoever does these things is an abomination to the Lord; and because of these abominable practices the Lord your God is driving them out before you. You shall be blameless before the Lord your God. For these nations, which you are about to dispossess, give heed to soothsayers and to diviners; but as for you, the Lord your God has not allowed you to do so" (Deuteronomy 18:9–14).

The giants, the progeny of demons, were once more in the land polluting the bloodline of man. As in the time of the Flood, they had to be destroyed.

"Hear, O Israel; you are to pass over the Jordan this day, to go in to dispossess nations greater and mightier than yourselves, cities great and fortified up to heaven, a people great and tall, the sons of Anakim, whom you know, and of whom you have heard it said, 'Who can stand before the sons of Anak?' Know therefore this day that he who goes over before you as a devouring fire is the Lord your God; he will destroy them and subdue them before you; so you shall drive them out, and make them perish quickly, as the Lord has promised you" (Deuteronomy 9:1–3).

The giants and the great cities in the land speak to us of the immensity of the iniquity that we all face and have to conquer. *"Do not defile yourselves by any of these things, for by all these the nations I am casting out before you defiled themselves; and the land became defiled, so that I punished its iniquity, and the land vomited out its inhabitants"* (Leviticus 18:24–25).

We know well that Israel failed God in countless ways, but even so he always wanted to have mercy upon them.

> *"But if they confess their iniquity and the iniquity of their fathers in their treachery which they committed against me, and also in walking contrary to me, so that I walked contrary to them and brought them into the land of their enemies; if then their uncircumcised heart is humbled and they make amends for their iniquity; then I will remember my covenant with Jacob, and I will remember my covenant with Isaac and my covenant with Abraham, and I will remember their land"* (Leviticus 26:40–42).

Sadly, their covenant did indeed become a curse to them, and still today they live under the results of their failure. The results of the iniquity in the Amorites led to child sacrifice (our practice of abortion is just as bad), and the iniquity in Sodom and Gomorrah led to the gross homosexual immorality for which those cities became a byword (and which is increasingly being authorised and accepted in Christian churches today). The prophets God sent unceasingly warned them (and us) of the inevitable judgement that God will accord to any society where unchecked iniquity and its consequences are tolerated.

Now we need to look at the words of the prophets to understand the working of iniquity in God's people. First, Isaiah and Jeremiah:

> *"Because of the iniquity of his covetousness I was angry, I smote him, I hid my face and was angry; but he went on backsliding in the way of his own heart"* (Isaiah 57:17).

> *"Behold the Lord's hand is not shortened, that it cannot save, or his ear dull that it cannot hear; but your iniquities have made a separation between you and your God, and your sins have hid his face from you so that he does not hear"* (Isaiah 59:1–2).

> *"It may be the house of Judah will hear all the evil which I intend to do to them, so that every one may turn from his evil way, and that I may forgive their iniquity and their sin"* (Jeremiah 36:3).

Now Ezekiel:

> *"Son of man, I have made you a watchman for the house of Israel; whenever you hear a word from my mouth, you shall give them warning from me. If I say to the wicked, 'You shall surely die,' and you give him no warning, nor speak to warn the wicked from his wicked way, in order to save his life, that wicked man shall die in his iniquity; but his blood I will require at your hand. But if you warn the wicked, and he does not turn from his wickedness, or from his wicked way, he shall die in his iniquity; but you will have saved your life. Again, if a righteous man turns from his righteousness, and commits iniquity, and I lay a stumbling block before him, he shall die; because you have not warned him, he shall die for his sin, and his righteous deeds which he has done shall not be remembered; but his blood will I require at your hand. Nevertheless, if you warn the righteous man not to sin, and he does not sin, he shall surely live, because he took warning; and you will have saved your life"* (Ezekiel 3:17–21; see also chapter 33).

> *"Son of man, these men have taken their idols into their hearts and set the stumbling block of iniquity before their faces; should I let myself be inquired of at all by them?* (Ezekiel 14:3).

> *"And the nations shall know that the house of Israel went into captivity for their iniquity, because they dealt so treacherously with me that I hid my face from them and gave them into the hand of their adversaries, and they all fell by the sword. I dealt with them according to their uncleanness and their transgressions, and hid my face from them"* (Ezekiel 39:23–24).

Daniel makes a significant contribution:

> "*As it is written in the book of Moses, all this calamity has come upon us, yet we have not entreated the favour of the Lord our God turning from our iniquities and giving heed to thy truth. Therefore the Lord has kept ready the calamity and brought it upon us; for the Lord our God is righteous in all the works which he has done and we have not obeyed his voice*" (Daniel 9:13–14).

> "*Seventy weeks of years are decreed concerning your people and your holy city, to finish the transgression, to put an end to sin, and to atone for iniquity, to bring in everlasting righteousness, to seal both vision and prophet and to anoint the most holy place*" (Daniel 9:24).

Then Hosea speaks out:

> "*The days of punishment have come, the days of recompense have come. The prophet is a fool, the man of spirit is mad, because of your great iniquity and great hatred. The prophet is the watchman of Ephraim, the people of my God, yet a fowler's snare is on all his way, and hatred in the house of his God. They have deeply corrupted themselves as in the days of Gibeah: he will remember their iniquity, he will punish their sins*" (Hosea 9:7–9).

> "*Return, O Israel, to the Lord your God, for you have stumbled because of your iniquity. Take with you words and return to the Lord; say to him, 'Take away all iniquity; accept that which is good and we will render the fruit of our lips'*" (Hosea 14:1–2).

Amos, the shepherd-prophet, declared, "*You only have I known of all the families of the earth; therefore I punish you for your iniquities*" (Amos 3:2).

The prophet Micah adds his voice: "*Who is a God like thee, pardoning iniquity and passing over transgression for the remnant of his inheritance? He does not retain his anger forever because he delights in steadfast love. He will again have compassion upon us: he will tread our iniquities under foot. Thou wilt cast our sins into the sea*" (Micah 7:18–19).

Zechariah speaks out: "*And the Lord said to Satan, 'The Lord rebuke you, O Satan! The Lord who has chosen Jerusalem rebuke you! Is this not a brand plucked from the fire?' Now Joshua was standing before the angel, clothed with filthy garments. And the angel said to those who were standing before him, 'Remove the filthy garments from him.' And to him he said, 'Behold, I have taken your iniquity away from you and I will clothe you with rich apparel'*" (Zechariah 3:2–4).

Malachi closes the Old Testament revelation in similar vein: "*My covenant with (Levi) was a covenant of life and peace, and I gave them to him that he might fear; and he feared me and stood in awe of my name. True instruction was in his mouth and no wrong was found on his lips. He walked with me in peace and uprightness, and he turned many from iniquity*" (Malachi 2:5–6).

It is from the Old Testament that we need to derive our abhorrence of iniquity. To have insight and understanding of this long history of man's failure and specifically Israel's failure is necessary for a full comprehension of God's provision of the New Covenant.

INIQUITY IS A HABIT

THE WOUNDS OF LIFE

REJECTION OF ALL KINDS, HOMELESSNESS, RAPE, WAR, HATRED, PHYSICAL & SEXUAL ABUSE, CULTURE SHOCK, POVERTY, SICKNESS, ACCIDENT, REDUNDANCY, ORPHAN, INJUSTICE, FEARFUL EXPERIENCES, FEAR, THE OCCULT, INSECURITY IN CHILDHOOD, PORNOGRAPHY, HOMOSEXUAL EXPERIENCE, ABORTION, DIVORCE, ASSAULT ON PERSON OR PROPERTY, FAILURE, MOCKERY, BAD REPUTATION, PRISON, DRUGS, PERVERSION, BANKRUPTCY, DECEPTION OF OTHERS

LEAD TO A PRISON OF THE MIND

FANTASY THINKING
BAD MEMORIES
HIDDEN DEPRESSION
UNDUE INTELLECTUALISM
(KNOWLEDGE/RESPECTABLE)
MENTAL COMPETITIION
IMPOVERISHED RELATIONSHIPS
SUPPRESSED EMOTIONS
REPRESSED FEELINGS

LEAD TO A PRISON OF EMOTIONS

DAMAGED/BRUISED/
OPPRESSED
ATTENTION SEEKING
LACK OF REALITY
MOOD SWINGS – SULKS/
DEPRESSION/EUPHORIA
DEPENDENT RELATIONSHIPS
IRRATIONAL FEARS
CRISIS CREATION
INCESSANT TALKING
OUTBURSTS OF RAGE
UNRELIABILITY

LEAD TO A PRISON OF THE BODY

UNCONTROLLABLE LUSTS
SEXUAL EXCESS
PHYSICAL ACHIEVEMENT
SUBSTANCE DEPENDENCY
EXTREMES OF APPETITE
HEDONISM - (PARTYING/
HOLIDAYS/LUXURY)
OVER CONCERN WITH
APPEARANCE/DRESS

THESE BRING AN INABILITY TO SUSTAIN REAL/WHOLE RELATIONSHIPS IN MARRIAGE, IN FAMILY, IN CHURCH AND IN SOCIETY

RECONCILIATION

Reconciliation between man and his Creator can only occur when the obstacle that separated them in the first place is removed. We must identify that obstacle accurately before it can be removed. We have seen that the introduction of iniquity into Adam's heart brought immediate separation from God. We have seen that the basis of that iniquity is "the lie" with which Satan has deceived the whole world (i.e. everybody in it) right up to the present time.

So much of our attempted ministry to the world proceeds from a wrong understanding of the issues that are involved. In the Garden of Eden, Satan, in his great wisdom, understood those issues very well. He knew that for man to live under "the lie," he must deliberately turn away from "the truth," which is God's Word. Today it is the reverse of that. For man to live under "the truth," he must deliberately turn away from "the lie" and back to God.

In our "post-Christian" society, there is no general recognition or acceptance of the God of the Bible and so we have no diagnosis of our problem. We have become a multi-faith society. Tolerance is simply a mask for refusing to acknowledge any absolute moral authority. The widely popular idea that all religions lead to the same God is not tolerance; it is ignorance compounded by carelessness. Today's popular materialism and hedonism have found a convenient way of saying that it does not matter what god (or gods) you decide to adopt because all have equal validity! Within this careless and undiscerning view, the conflicting claims of monotheistic Christianity, Islam, and Judaism are considered to be sufficiently similar to warrant them making common cause over social issues and even some religious ones! But Christ alone delivers us from iniquity.

Along with the God-given right of free will to choose how he lives, man is given great responsibility. Irresponsible man, however, chooses to ignore that: thinking himself unaccountable and therefore free to live for himself alone. Because God is unchanging, it remains true today as ever that, *"God will by no means clear the guilty!"* Whether we like it or not, we *are* individually responsible for the choices we make and also for their outcome. Almighty God will require us to answer to him for all of them.

> *"Ever since the creation of the world his invisible nature, namely, his power and deity, has been clearly perceived in the things that have been made. So (men) are without excuse"* (Romans 1:20).

The rational arguments of the humanist, atheist, and agnostic will be found to be no defence on the day on which they will give account of themselves.

"By faith we understand that the world was created by the word of God, so that what is seen is made out of things which do not appear . . . and without faith it is impossible to please him. For whoever would draw near to God must believe that he exists and that he rewards those who seek him" (Hebrews 11:3, 6).

"The God who made the world and everything in it, being Lord of heaven and earth, does not live in shrines made by man, nor is he served by human hands as if he has need of anything, since he himself gives to all men life and breath and everything. And he made from one every nation of men to live on the face of the earth, having determined allotted periods and the boundaries of their habitation, that they should seek God, in the hope that they might feel after him and find him . . . The times of ignorance God overlooked, but now he commands all men everywhere to repent, because he has fixed a day on which he will judge the world in righteousness by a man he has appointed, and of this he has given assurance by raising him from the dead" (Acts 17:24–27, 30–31).

No other faith makes such a devastating claim upon the lives of all men. It is man's duty to seek for God. He is intellectually equipped to do it. He has the responsibility to evaluate the evidence presented by the world's religions, not just to follow blindly after authorities and powers. Our evangelism must present this choice in its starkest terms. Will men deliberately continue to live in spiritual darkness, thus serving Satan, or will they turn to the God of the Bible, our Creator, and, seeking after truth, find the wonderful salvation offered in Jesus Christ?

Satan and his hosts are at great pains to divert our attention to anything other than "the truth," which alone can set man free from his darkness. Religion has no power to change men's hearts, but without such a change it is impossible to be reconciled to the holy God.

Religion can never describe the covenant relationship a disciple of Christ enjoys with God. It truly is a profound relationship far deeper that that existing between a human father and his son.

This covenant relationship is no agreement based upon religious sentiment; the terms of the covenant made through Jesus Christ, by which we are reconciled to him, are just as severe and demanding as the terms of the Old Covenant but they take us to a higher level spiritually. We must obey him, not as a legal requirement, but because such obedience is the inevitable consequence of loving him. If we do not obey him in all things, it is plain that we do not love him and deception still continues in our life.

Newborn Christians are just like Cain was in his day, except that they are now saved by God's grace. Their iniquity is still in them. We still hate one another. We still rebel. We still have unclean thoughts. We are still horrified to discover lust lurking deep inside us. But despite it all we are reconciled to God through Jesus Christ by his grace.

Jesus' primary command that we love one another as he has loved us exposes the thoughts of our hearts, for we find that we cannot do it. The love we have for one another is the evidence for our salvation. That is how God has remade us because reconciliation with God opens the door for reconciliation with each other. Jesus sought unity among his disciples that could only be achieved by removing the iniquity from their hearts and the sin from their lives. To be reconciled to one another in this sense, men must first be reconciled to God.

Then begins the process of *becoming* love, as we learn to truly love one another. This comes neither naturally nor easily. It involves self-denial and the laying down of our preferred way of life. Man's love of independence is natural to him. Such independence frequently becomes a habit of life that suits him (so he thinks!) and so he is reluctant to give it up.

Our unwillingness to recognise a need for intimate (nonsexual) relationships arises directly from iniquity. It is only as we recognise the source in our heart that we can make progress in dealing with it.

Jesus has provided a safe environment so that this deep work of the Spirit can mature in us:

1. Discipleship
2. Christian marriage
3. Church family

Personal discipleship was part of God's provision for this growth to exist and develop. Marriage was a further part, as was church life—the interplay of relationships within God's family. All were, and are, safe environments for God to perfect us in love. But reconciliation needs both parties to be equally committed to the process for it to work. Discipleship does not work effectively unless there is a group of disciples committed to one another; the church family cannot develop beyond the commitment that the parties are willing to make to the body. Christian marriage cannot work without the total commitment of each partner to the principles of discipleship and to the Word of God.

What am *I* getting out of this? is a question that reflects the iniquitous attitude of so many in today's visible church. The attitude should rather be, "What is the Lord saying I should bring to this?"

Our churches are bedevilled with pragmatism and halfheartedness. These, along with scepticism, are fruit of the flesh life. Speaking the truth in love is nonexistent: criticism rules unchecked.

Being transformed into the likeness of Christ is a process of inner change that will inevitably bring a change of lifestyle with it. As we increasingly become love, we increasingly love and increasingly serve. When this happens in a family, as God intends, the mutuality of care and service prevents one party from being burned out. Where such mutuality does not exist, individual demands for care and attention will overwhelm the others involved. The safeguard is Jesus' insistence that all are to be disciples. He did not commit himself to those who were not disciples, nor did he grant them intimacy (John 2:24–25). This should caution us to exercise discernment.

The two necessities for our growth to spiritual maturity are:

1. Acknowledging unconditionally that we are disciples of Jesus. Where applicable, our marriage and our home life will also reflect this.
2. Being part of a church of disciples, knowing ourselves to be God's family, with whom we share in worship.

While we are to be outward looking and ready to serve others in need, we are to be discerning in the level of commitment we enter into with individuals. In this regard, the more mature brothers and sisters have a high level of responsibility in their church to lead by example and encourage the less mature, for while we can and must forgive everyone who requires it, there can be no true reconciliation with people who themselves resist change.

INIQUITY IN THE NEW TESTAMENT

It is helpful to see where iniquity occurs in the New Testament, even though modern translations may not use the word. It's there all right! The word *adikia* (without righteousness) and its close relatives, occurs sixty-eight times. The word family of *anomia* (without law) occur twenty-six times. The word *amartia* and its close relatives (sin and sinner) occur 269 times. This last word is normally used to describe the doing of wrong things that need forgiveness, although it may also be used occasionally for the condition of sin (or iniquity) as in the Old Testament.

Paul also uses the word *amartia* in Romans chapters 5, 6 and 7 to describe the terrible spiritual condition we are all in and how Jesus has saved us out of it. Paul's analysis reveals the distinction between the "old man" (how we were, dominated by the flesh) and the "new man" (how we are, when led by the Spirit through faith in Jesus Christ).

Wouldn't it be wonderful if when we are born again, we found that everything about us was new and fresh? Some preachers lead people to believe that this is how it is. Then, with the passage of a little time, disillusionment sets in because we find the reality to be rather different! The unpalatable truth is that we find that we are still troubled by much of the baggage from our past. We realise that the way we lived was wrong, and we want to live a new life as a believer and follower of Jesus, and yet we find that the old habits, attitudes, and behaviour patterns are still there holding us back. Is something wrong with us?

No, not at all! Our experience is common to all believers. Take a look at Romans 7 and you will see that you are in very good company! Paul tells it like it is!

Salvation surely brings new birth by the Holy Spirit, but the situation is rather like it is for a man who has just taken a hot bath. He is completely clean from head to toe, but discovers he is dressed in someone else's dirty old clothes! If he has any sense, he wishes to be rid of those as fast as possible because, although he might be scrubbed clean, he smells like a drain and looks equally disgusting!

God has given us the task and responsibility to put our salvation into effect in our own being, body, and lifestyle. Just as the people of Israel were brought out of Egypt by God's power, and then had to take the Promised Land by fighting for it, so we are brought to new life by the sovereign power of God, and then have to take control of every part of our being by fighting for it. The parallel is precise and the purpose is similar. In their struggle to subdue the Promised Land, the Israelites would learn discipline, how to depend on God, and discover an understanding of their own strength.

We have seen that the land of Canaan was occupied by nations completely dominated by iniquity. Consequently, they were not only hostile to God but were extremely wicked. Their condition is the same as it was for each one of us before we were saved. Our souls and bodies were completely dominated by iniquity. We could not think, speak, or live truth. Rather, we were (and still are) dominated by "the lie" of Satan. The difference is that our past has been forgiven (and forgotten!) so we have been accepted by God and reconciled to him. He has put his Holy Spirit into us, so the power is there within us to bring our body, mind, and spirit into God's order. That order is revealed in God's Word.

Paul uses the picture of putting off the old and putting on the new (Ephesians 4:22; Colossians 3:8–9). It is as if we are in a continual process of replacing bits of our old, filthy clothing with new bits that are pure. There is a wonderful picture of this given us by Zechariah in the Old Testament.

> *"Then he showed me Joshua the High Priest standing before the angel of the Lord, and Satan standing at his right hand to accuse him. And the Lord said to Satan, 'The Lord rebuke you, O Satan! The Lord, who has chosen Jerusalem, rebuke you! Is this not a brand plucked from the fire?' Now Joshua was standing before the angel, clothed with filthy garments. And the angel said to those who were standing before him, 'Remove the filthy garments from him.' And to him he said, 'Behold I have taken your iniquity away from you, and I will clothe you with rich apparel.' And I said, 'Let them put a clean turban on his head.' So they put a clean turban on his head and clothed him with garments; and the angel of the Lord was standing by"* (Zechariah 3:1–5).

John uses this same picture in Revelation as one of God's promises to those who are overcomers. *"Yet I have still a few names in Sardis, people who have not soiled their garments; and they shall walk with me in white, for they are worthy. He who conquers shall be clad thus in white garments and I will not block his name out of the book of life"* (Revelation 3:4–5).

In this case, John suggests that in salvation we receive a white robe (of righteousness) from God and it is now our responsibility to ensure that it does not get soiled through unrighteous behaviour. Since we know that the root of all unrighteousness is iniquity in the heart, we discover the contrast between those who keep their robes clean and those who do not. Those who learn how to deal with the iniquity in their heart and the sin in their lives are contrasted with those who do not. The churches of Revelation were in just such a condition. They were saved people, but they were not dealing with their hidden iniquity under the terms of the covenant God had made with them, and this had serious consequences.

There are many examples of this condition in the New Testament:

> *"Not every one who says to me 'Lord! Lord!' will enter the kingdom of heaven, but he who does the will of my Father who is in heaven. On that day many will say to me, 'Lord, Lord, did we not prophesy in your name, and cast out demons in your name, and do many mighty works in your name?' And then will I declare to them, 'I never knew you; depart from me, you workers of iniquity (Greek: anomia)'"* (Matthew 7:21–23).

> *"And someone said to him, 'Lord, will those who are saved be few?' And he said to them, 'Strive to enter by the narrow door; for many I tell you, will seek to enter and will not be able. When once the householder has risen up and shut the door, you will begin to stand outside and to knock at the door, saying, "Lord, open to us." He will answer you, "I do not know where you come from." Then you will begin to say, "We ate and drank in your presence, and you taught in our streets." But he will say, "I tell you, I do not know where you come from; depart from me, all you workers of iniquity (Greek: adikia)!"'"* (Luke 13:23–27).

> *"Woe to you, scribes and Pharisees, hypocrites! For you cleanse the outside of the cup and of the plate, but inside they are full of extortion and rapacity. You blind Pharisee! First cleanse the inside of the cup and of*

the plate, that the outside also may be clean. Woe to you, scribes and Pharisees, hypocrites! For you are like whitewashed tombs, which outwardly appear beautiful, but within they are full of dead men's bones and all uncleanness. So you also appear outwardly righteous to men, but within you are full of hypocrisy and iniquity (Greek: anomia)" (Matthew 23:25–28).

"And because iniquity (Greek: anomia) is multiplied, most men's love shall grow cold" (Matthew 24:12).

"Repent therefore of this wickedness of yours, and pray to the Lord that, if possible, the intent of your heart may be forgiven you. For I see that you are in the gall of bitterness and in the bond of iniquity (Greek: adikia)" (Acts 8:22–23).

"Blessed are those whose iniquities (Greek: anomia) are forgiven, and whose sins (Greek: amartia) are covered" (Romans 4:7).

"I am speaking in human terms, because of your natural limitations (lit: weakness of the flesh). For just as you once yielded your members to impurity and to greater and greater iniquity (Greek: anomia), so now yield your members to righteousness for sanctification" (Romans 6:19).

"Thou hast loved righteousness and hated iniquity (Greek: anomia); therefore thy God hath anointed thee with the oil of gladness beyond thy comrades" (Hebrews 1:9).

"Then he adds, 'I will remember their sins and their iniquities (Greek: anomia) no more. And where there is forgiveness of these, there is no longer any offering for sins (Greek: amartia)" (Hebrews 10:17–18).

"Come out of her, my people, lest you take part in her sins, lest you share in her plagues; for her sins are heaped high as heaven, and God has remembered her iniquities (Greek: adikia)" (Revelation 18:4–5).

The shocking revelation that is given us under the terms of the New Covenant is that *we* must take responsibility for dealing with all that is unrighteous in us. The notion that we are footloose and fancy free from the moment we become Christians is an utter delusion. It has led to libertarianism on a huge scale, with believers presuming on the mercy of God and living in a fashion that is scarcely different from the world. Disciples *are* free—but free to obey Christ, not free to please ourselves.

Every unclean thought or imagination; every unclean word that passes our lips; every selfish action or inaction; every sin; everything in our lives that falls below God's standard calls for action on our part. This is not unreasonable, because Jesus has made it possible for us to deal with it. After all, he has filled us with his Spirit. Some believe that once they are saved they are free of responsibility for sin and iniquity. They are not.

"For if we sin deliberately after receiving the knowledge of the truth, there no longer remains a sacrifice for sins, but a fearful prospect of judgment, and a fury of fire which will consume the adversaries. A man who has violated the law of Moses dies without mercy at the testimony of two or three witnesses. How much worse punishment do you think will be deserved by the man who has spurned the Son of God, and profaned the blood of the covenant by which he was sanctified, and outraged the Spirit of grace?" (Hebrews 10:26–29).

"Since we have these promises, beloved, let us cleanse ourselves from every defilement of body and spirit, and make holiness perfect in the fear of God" (2 Corinthians 7:1).

How are we to do this?

REPENTANCE, RENEWAL, AND RESISTANCE

We have seen that every man has inherited from Adam a violent, selfish, and greedy independence of God. Repentance—our willing submission to our Creator and his revealed will for us—wonderfully reverses the otherwise irrevocable choice that Adam made on our behalf. As we have seen, it is because of Jesus and through him alone that we have such an option.

Salvation without a total submission to the whole of God's will and Word is not salvation at all. It is an endeavour to negotiate the terms of God's covenant in order that we can preserve something of our independent lifestyle. It is a futile endeavour.

Everything we are as unregenerate humans is repugnant to God. Only a carefully considered recognition of our fallen condition can lead to that deep and true repentance, which brings death to the old way and opens the door to the new. Because we live in an age when so much is instantly available, we have formed the mistaken impression that coming back to God is an instant business. Any suggestion that salvation in its fullest sense is a *process* is rejected out of hand. Amongst other false beliefs it has encouraged the idea of "once saved, always saved." This dangerous notion is entirely consistent with the "instant society" in which we live. The truth is that a disciple of Christ *has been* saved, he *is being* saved, and he *will be* saved. We are so used to achieving instant responses and instant solutions that we can make these initial steps in salvation superficial and in the end of little value. Repentance is our first response to the gospel of Christ, but many see it quite wrongly as a momentary thing that, once expressed, needs no further attention or repetition! There are many in our churches today with no understanding of repentance in the deep spiritual sense that Jesus desires, often because they never repented properly in the first place. "*I had heard of thee by the hearing of the ear, but now my eye sees thee; therefore I despise myself, and repent in dust and ashes*" (Job 42:6).

The repentance shown to us in the Old Testament is a turning back to God for his mercy on account of our many sins. Repentance in the New Testament emphasises a radical change of mind: coming to your senses after careful consideration. When a person understands his true position as a rebel against God, he will surely exercise good sense and come back to God. That is the process of biblical repentance. Job, when confronted by God's majesty, recognised his own intrinsic unrighteousness (iniquity).

> "'*Yet even now,' says the Lord, 'return to me with all your heart, with fasting, with weeping, and with mourning; rend your hearts and not your garments.' Return to the Lord, your God, for he is gracious and merciful, slow to anger, and abounding in steadfast love, and repents of evil*" (Joel 2:12–13).

Joel says that it must also be a change of heart that goes beyond the intellectual. Our whole person surrenders to God's will—on our knees. It is body, mind, and emotions yielding to the holy Creator in a first response to his command and his declaration of love.

> *"Now when they heard this, they were cut to the heart and said to Peter and the rest of the apostles, 'Brethren, what shall we do?' And Peter said to them, 'Repent and be baptised every one of you in the name of Jesus Christ for the forgiveness of your sins and you shall receive the gift of the Holy Spirit. For the promise is to you and your children and to all who are far off, every one whom the Lord our God calls to him"* (Acts 2:37–39).

This was Peter's reply at Pentecost to those who first came under conviction of their need to have their sins forgiven. It has always been the starting place for those who would be saved. Ongoing repentance in the life of the believer is not so that he might be saved again because that is impossible. It is much broader and more informed. It is this repentance that deals not only with sins but also with the iniquity of the heart.

When Jesus examines the seven churches in Revelation 2 and 3, he calls five of them to "repent." The two who do not receive this injunction are suffering persecution for their faith. In a way these seven churches may be considered to be a generalised picture of the Christian Church worldwide at any given time. Persecution of believers has gone on from the very beginning and it is in the world today. However, the vast majority of Christian churches are not under persecution and are thus free to follow their faith in a practically uninhibited environment. However, it seems that such liberty does not sit well with the churches. It is soon turned into carelessness and licence. History shows plainly that the true church thrives in times of persecution while those not wholeheartedly committed to the truth fall away under pressure to conform and compromise with organised religion and the ways of the world.

The call to the five churches to "repent" gives us cause to think about what Jesus is saying here. Clearly those churches are made up of many believers. They are Christians who would fully expect to go to heaven when the Lord comes for his bride. But what do we find? Once more, we discover that there is a cost for those in the churches who are not "conquerors." The promises that Jesus is making are all to those who conquer. For those who do not conquer some disturbing issues are raised.

Just as during his earthly ministry, Jesus seems to be raising the spectre of a double standard existing amongst God's people. Two distinct groups are described in the parable of the "wheat" and the "tares" (Matthew 13). As he showed then, the two will grow together until the time of the end when the reapers will distinguish between them for the first time. It seems that there will be many shocked and disappointed believers on that Day.

Jesus said of his coming, *"One will be taken and one will be left"* (Luke 17:34–35). The question is, who are those to be left behind? The answer is to be found in Revelation 7:9–17:

> *"After this I looked, and behold, a great multitude which no man could number, from every nation, from all tribes and peoples and tongues, standing before the throne and the Lamb, clothed in white robes, with palm branches in their hands, and crying out with a loud voice, "Salvation belongs to our God who sits upon the throne, and to the Lamb!" And all the angels stood round the throne and round the elders and the four living creatures, and they fell on their faces before the throne and worshipped God, saying, "Amen! Blessing and glory and wisdom and thanksgiving and honour and power and might be to our God for ever and ever! Amen." Then one of the elders addressed me, saying, "Who are these, clothed in white robes, and whence have they come?" I said to him, "Sir, you know." And he said to me, "These are they who have come out of great tribulation, they have washed their robes and made them white in the blood of the Lamb. Therefore are they*

before the throne of God, and serve him day and night within his temple; and he who sits on the throne will shelter them with his presence. They shall hunger no more, neither thirst any more; the sun shall not strike them, nor any scorching heat. For the Lamb in the midst of the throne will be their shepherd, and he will guide them to springs of living water; and God will wipe away every tear from their eyes."

Please note how many there are in this group! Please note where these good folk are *standing* in heaven! Now look at the rewards promised to the conquerors in the Sardis church: *"Yet you have still a few names in Sardis, people who have not soiled their garments; and they shall walk with me in white, for they are worthy. He who conquers shall be clad thus in white garments, and I will not blot his name out of the book of life; I will confess his name before my Father and before his angels"* (Revelation 3:4–5).

Many had soiled the robe of righteousness given them at the time of their salvation. How can this be? For an understanding of the mystery we can look elsewhere in Scripture:

"And convince some who doubt; save some by snatching them out of the fire; on some even have mercy with fear, hating even the garment spotted by the flesh" (Jude 1: 22–23). *"And the angel said to those who were standing before him, 'Remove the filthy garments from him.' And to him he said, 'Behold, I have taken your iniquity away from you, and I will clothe you with rich apparel'"* (Zechariah 3:4).

We see then that the multitude standing before the throne were believers (saved people) who had never succeeded in dealing with their iniquity. Inevitably they continued to live a fleshly life. They may well have been sincere but they were not disciples. They did not and could not subject themselves to the discipline of the Word and were in danger of having their names blotted out of the Book of Life altogether. They were not raptured on the day of the Lord, and instead had to pass through that terrible time of the Great Tribulation that will come upon all those who the Lord does not take away with him. We are looking at one of the major tragedies of all time. Jesus called them to "repent" as the first step of dealing with the issues that he was showing them, but the number that failed to heed his warning is beyond counting.

By God's grace alone these people have been received into heaven, but only as through the trial of that Great Tribulation, where they washed their robes clean at last. They stand before God's throne with the promise that never again will they experience such a trauma as they have passed through. It is over. But they have missed the best that God had intended for them.

"He who conquers, I will grant him to sit with me on my throne, as I myself conquered and sat down with my Father on his throne" (Revelation 3:21). Those who have soiled their robes do not *sit* on God's throne as a joint heir with Jesus. They *stand* before that throne, which is wonderful, but sitting on the throne is better. The conqueror, at one with Jesus on earth, will be at one with him forever. Those who build with gold, silver, or precious stones will have their reward (but in heaven!) when he comes. Those who build with wood, hay, or straw will suffer a dreadful loss—saved, but only as through fire. (See 1 Corinthians 3:11–15.)

"Repent!" is the cry of Jesus to his church all down the ages. *"Remember then what you received and heard; keep that and repent. If you will not awake (or watch), I will come like a thief, and you will not know at what hour I have come upon you"* (Revelation 3:3).

The Watchmen must teach that repentance leading to renewal is to be part of our daily Christian walk as disciples of Jesus.

It will be helpful to you to study the illustrations at the end of this chapter. They are designed as aids to reinforce this vital matter and to lead you into a practical response.

Repentance is always the first stage in our transformation from being a son of Adam (as we were born in the flesh) to being a son of God (as we were later born by the Spirit). Just as it is the first appropriate response to hearing the gospel, so it is the appropriate continuing response to hearing Jesus' words to us as his disciples.

Without repentance, there can be no change in us. Our outward behaviour can be modified to some extent by an effort of our will, but the inward man—our character—will remain the same. Repentance does not signal a defeat but a victory, but it is only possible when we have fully understood its nature and purpose.

In repentance, we stop making excuses. We stop blaming others for who we are. We stop complaining about our circumstances. We face up to the truth and now, as sons of God, we step right up and take full responsibility. People blame God and they blame the devil in the same breath. We may have had appalling circumstances to cope with, but now we have a new identity. We are in an entirely new situation because God is our Father and we are no longer bound to the devil by the iniquity of our old man. By repentance, we put him off; we cast him away like a smelly, soiled garment because we are clean and we are going to put on that wonderful, bright, clean robe of righteousness.

Many are tempted to hold back something when it comes to repentance. We have a desire to let the hidden things remain hidden. But this is Satan's trap. As we confess every unclean thing residing in our hearts, we are taking ground from the devil. How he longs to hang on to something in us.

Judas was an unconfessed thief and when the moment came Satan could enter him and use him to betray Jesus. Holding on to unconfessed sins and iniquity leaves the believer in a dangerous situation and extremely vulnerable to the devil's infiltrations.

We are talking of "sanctification" here. Admittedly it is a technical term but that must not frighten us away! Because of widespread error, it is important to be clear in our thinking. We are justified through faith at the moment of our new birth. As we have seen, our new birth is the beginning of a new life. It is the first stage in a long process that will last until we die. It is not an end in itself. Justification by God's grace is what enables God to accept us even as we go on being changed into his likeness through sanctification. Justification is a permanent state of grace; we have been made perfect yet at the same time we are *being* made perfect! The image of a baby growing up is apt to illustrate this. We do not expect a baby to take adult responsibilities, but neither do we expect adults to behave like babies. There is right behaviour expected from each stage of growth to maturity. So by God's grace we are "acceptable in the beloved" even as we are working out our salvation day by day.

At first, repentance opened the door of our heart to justification because in repenting we put off our natural rebellion against God and sought for the forgiveness of our past sins. So, for the believer, that is in the past. But repentance *keeps* the door of our heart open to receive new life as we actively continue to put off any iniquity that the Holy Spirit uncovers (*cf* Revelation 3:20—a passage commonly applied to *un*believers, but in fact addressed to believers!).

Justification credits us with Jesus' righteousness. The Father has imputed it to us and we are fully covered and protected by it. However, as we continue the fight to live in obedience to Jesus, we are changed increasingly to conform to his character. This is the process of sanctification. But, if we wilfully suspend this process, we are in trouble.

It seems that in this case we are deliberately soiling that precious white robe of justification that has been freely given to us. When that happens God can do nothing with us. It is just as if we have terminated our own discipleship. Has our justification then become invalid? Who can answer that question? Only the day of the Lord will reveal it.

"For it is impossible to restore again to repentance those who have once been enlightened, who have tasted the heavenly gift, who have become partakers of the Holy Spirit, and who have tasted the goodness of the word of God, and the powers of the age to come, if they then commit apostasy, since they crucify the Son of God on their own account and hold him up to contempt. For land which has drunk the rain that often falls upon it, and brings forth vegetation useful to those for whose sake it is cultivated receives a blessing from God, but if it bears thorns and thistles it is worthless and near to being cursed; its end is to be burned" (Hebrews 6:4–8).

The point I make is simply this: iniquity must be killed (put to death). It can never be cleaned up. It will never remain dormant. It can never be hidden. If there is one drop left anywhere in us it will rise up again like a flood to take possession of us.

We must kill it ourselves, by our own deliberate choice and in complete agreement with God's Word!

"Now this I affirm and testify in the Lord, that you must no longer live as the Gentiles do, in the futility of their minds; they are darkened in their understanding, alienated from the life of God because of the ignorance that is in them, due to their hardness of heart; they have become callous and have given themselves up to licentiousness, greedy to practice every kind of uncleanness. You did not so learn Christ! – assuming that you have heard about him and were taught in him, as the truth is in Jesus. Put off your old nature which belongs to your former manner of life and is corrupt through deceitful lusts, and be renewed in the spirit of your minds, and put on the new nature, created after the likeness of God in true righteousness and holiness" (Ephesians 4:17–24).

There is an order in this process. The first thing that happens in the heart is conviction. This is insight given us by our loving Father. It is the Holy Spirit showing us that change is needed. Then the mind, which has previously been hostile to God, agrees with the Spirit. It is a change of mind made possible only in the power of the Spirit. The emotions and feelings are involved as, conscious of God's presence, we are ready to kneel and speak to him even with tears. This is confession. There is no need to rush. Since we are not under condemnation, we are able to explore the whole situation as the Holy Spirit sheds his light on it. We are able to look back in time and see how we have offended and been offended. We are able to see what hurts we have caused to others. We see, often for the first time, how unutterably selfish and self-centred we are. We can put it all off because we no longer need it or want it in our lives.

We are protected in this painful process by our relationship with Jesus and his with us, for he has promised he will never leave us nor forsake us. There is no condemnation anymore: Jesus has paid the price. That is settled in heaven. So we do not need to defend ourselves for there is nothing to be defended. We have all the time in the world to allow the process to take its course. Even when it hurts us we will accept the pain, just as Jesus did, and trust him for the outcome.

The need to confess and ask forgiveness from others is an important part of this process, as is the making of restitution where possible. But sensitivity is required so that we do not exacerbate a situation that may have already been dealt with by someone else. We cannot *demand* reconciliation with another person. We can only do our own part and leave them to do theirs.

We may have difficulty in recognising the "new man" in us. Indeed the world about us may fail to recognise it entirely. However, we are to live according to God's Word and not according to men's opinions. If through the Bible God says you are the new man, then you are the new man no matter what your doubts and outward appearance try to dictate. It is very important to recognise and confess what God has done for us, to us, and in us. Through faith we are transformed by the renewal of our mind so that we understand and appreciate who we are. We *were* of this world, now we are of the next world. Unless we believe and enter into the truth of our new birth by faith we can never receive the full benefit of it. Most of us have been governed for so long by our feelings and emotions that it has become an ingrained habit. We depend upon them! However, these are entirely unreliable and we must replace them by the Word of God. Even the renewal of our mind requires repentance. We must kill the old, iniquitous patterns of thinking. We must put to death memories, fantasies, and attitudes derived from the Tree of Knowledge. Until we have thoroughly dealt with them before the Lord, they will continue to plague us. *"Put to death, therefore, whatever belongs to your earthly nature . . ."* (Colossians 3:5). *"For though we live in the world we are not carrying on a worldly war, for the weapons of our warfare are not worldly but have divine power to destroy strongholds. We destroy arguments and every proud obstacle to the knowledge of God, and take every thought captive to obey Christ, being ready to punish every disobedience, when your obedience is complete"* (2 Corinthians 10:3–6).

We shall be faced with complex issues. For instance, indulgence in gross sexual immorality or pornography may not only attack and destroy us mentally, but also emotionally and physically. Because it affects all levels, it has to be tackled on all levels at the same time. Furthermore, it will generally require the help of an older brother or sister to finally lay it in the dust. Where we have wilfully opened ourselves up to iniquity, the devil has a stronghold on that area we have yielded to his tempting. Knowingly doing evil is essentially an act of worship—giving ourselves to the service of the devil. There is a dreadful cost involved.

Sanctification ultimately recovers the whole person from the clutches of the enemy so that he has nothing in us, and therefore has no power over us. That was the secret of Jesus' victory over Satan in the wilderness. There was no ground for the devil to invade! The indwelling power of Christ enables *us* to emulate that wonderful success! Hallelujah! *"May the God of peace himself sanctify you wholly; and may your spirit and soul and body be kept sound and blameless at the coming of our Lord Jesus Christ. He who calls you is faithful, and he will do it."* (1 Thessalonians 5:23–24).

7 NECESSARY STEPS IN THE PROCESS OF REPENTANCE LEADING TO RECONCILIATION WITH GOD AND EACH OTHER & GIVING US SELF CONTROL

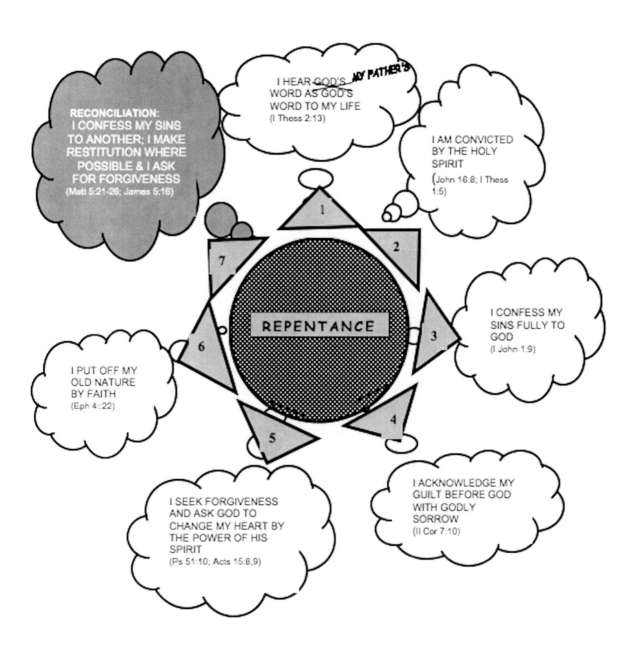

5 ELEMENTS OF SPIRITUAL RENEWAL FOR THE SON OF GOD

(CHANGES MY HEART)
(CHANGES MY BODY, SOUL & SPIRIT)
(CHANGES MY MIND, CHARACTER & LIFESTYLE)
(CHANGES MY RELATIONSHIPS)

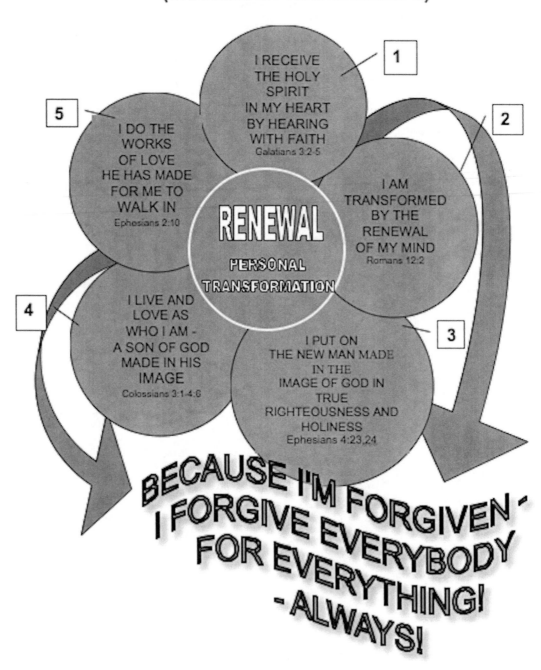

PUTTING ON THE NEW MAN

Paul says that the new man is, *"created after the likeness of God in true righteousness and holiness"* (Ephesians 4:24). That is who we are as sons of God.

There is no equivocation about such a statement. It is the reason why John says:

*"See what love the Father has given us, that we should be called children of God; and so we are. The reason the world does not know us is that it did not know him. Beloved we are God's children now; it does not yet appear what we shall be, but we know that when he appears we shall be like him, for we shall see him as he is. And every one who thus hopes in him purifies himself as he is pure. Everyone who commits **sin** is guilty of **iniquity; sin** is **iniquity**. You know that he appeared to take away **sins**, and in him there is no **sin**. No one who abides in him **sins**; no one who **sins** has either seen him or known him. Little children, let no one deceive you. He who does right is righteous, as he is righteous. He who commits **sin** is of the devil; for the devil has **sinned** from the beginning. The reason the Son of God appeared was to destroy the works of the devil. No one born of God commits **sin** for God's nature abides in him, and he cannot **sin**, because he is born of God. By this it may be seen who are the children of God, and who are the children of the devil: whoever does not do right is not of God, nor he who does not love his brother"* (1 John 3:1–10)

In the above quotation, I have taken the liberty of differentiating between iniquity and sin. This reflects accurately the use of the different Greek words, *amartia* (sin) and *anomia* (iniquity).

John practically summarises the Pauline doctrines of justification and sanctification. He shows that they are necessary to each other and will be revealed in us by the way we behave with and toward each other. True purity is very practical. Unless it identifies itself in love relationships with those around us it is not the real thing.

Renewal does not cause us to stand out in this world. We will not necessarily be successful, or admired or wanted by others. But often in difficult circumstances we shall increasingly live in the peace, joy and love that comes with sanctification.

John properly comments on the mundane appearance of God's children in the world, but there is an incredible glorification to come, when our appearance too will be changed and we shall look like Jesus as he is now. *"Lo! I tell you a mystery. We shall not all sleep, but we shall all be changed, in a moment, in the twinkling of an eye, at the last trumpet. For the trumpet will sound, and the dead will be raised imperishable, and we shall be changed"* (1 Corinthians 15: 51–52).

Until then, we are being changed inside. On that glorious day, our outward appearance will match our inner glory, for we shall be like Jesus in every respect. What this means is that we are becoming "love"; we are becoming "light"; we are becoming "holy." As we put off all the old, both bad and good, we put on Christ. We retain our unique personality, but we increasingly become like our Father in character. *"Since we have these promises, beloved, let us cleanse ourselves from every defilement of body and spirit and make holiness perfect in the fear of God"* (2 Corinthians 7:1). *"As obedient children, do not be conformed to the passions of your former ignorance, but as he who calls you is holy, be holy yourselves in all your conduct; since it is written, 'You shall be holy, for I am holy'"* (1 Peter 1:14–16).

Most Christians are taught that they are sinners and will always be sinners. Thus, they can never be holy as God is holy. This is a denial of our salvation and denies the power of the blood of the Lamb to change us. So many are taught a lie, often with the best of intentions, by those who do not know the power of God's Word to change them, because they personally have not understood "sanctification" and are not living as a disciple. Christians who think like this never know who they are, nor who their real Father is. They are Christian orphans. They worship and pray to an Old Covenant God. Like the Jews, they are subject to the elemental spirits and they constantly yield to the iniquity within. Leaders, knowing no better themselves, condone the passions of the flesh and in vain try to reconcile it to Scripture. Such a mixture of ignorance and unbelief in God's covenant of grace leads to loss of faith, hopelessness, despair, and practices of empty religious activities.

By the good confession of the truth of God's Word as his sons, we are renewed in our minds. As disciples of Jesus we are transformed in our usual patterns of behaviour and in our relationships. A change in lifestyle and true holiness follows. This is our spiritual worship.

IT IS CRUCIAL TO OUR RENEWAL (SANCTIFICATION) THAT WE STOP BEING WHAT WE ARE NOT!

"I AM A SON OF GOD I AM NO LONGER WHO I WAS"

IN REPENTANCE I PUT OFF WHO I WAS IN RENEWAL I AFFIRM WHO I AM

"I AM NO LONGER SUBJECT TO MY PAST, OR TO MY FLESH NATURE, OR TO MY CULTURE"

"BECAUSE OF JESUS IN ME, - I AM A CONQUEROR"

DISCIPLESHIP:
A CHALLENGE TO SPRITUAL MATURITY
FOR EVERY CHURCH AND ITS LEADERS

'Father, I pray that they may be one; even as you are in me and I in you, that they may be in us, so that the world may believe that you have sent me. The glory that you have given me I have given to them, that they may be one even as we are one, I in them and you in me, that they may become perfectly one, so that the world may know that you have sent me and that you have loved them even as you loved me' (John 17:21–23).

This passionate prayer of Jesus expresses his heart that his followers would be "one" with himself and his Father, and that this profound spiritual intimacy would be shared among his followers in the future. The prayer was offered in order that Christians, as children of God, might be clearly recognisable by the world as being different: men and women functioning as God's unique family community. Their love for each other would provide a demonstration of God's love that was available to all mankind.

The memory of the Last Supper, when he had initiated the New Covenant, would have been strong in Jesus' mind as he prayed. He knew well that his prayer could only be answered at the price of his own propitiating death and the consequent sending of the Holy Spirit. The new blood covenant, opening the door for the full reconciliation of man with God, was about to be established.

The apostles had the forbidding task of making this New Covenant known to the Jews who, seeking to maintain the Old Covenant, had already rejected Jesus in person. The "oneness" of the apostles would be a major factor in the success of this task.

At first it seemed easy. The power of God was evident in all they did, and people were amazed to see what was going on. The Holy Spirit was manifestly active among the believers. But always there were problems.

The Book of Acts tells the tale of disputes and compromise arising among believers even in those early days, and all the epistles carry accounts of problems in the churches. The heart of man is not easily changed. Ananias and Sapphira provide an early but very clear example of that (see Acts 5:1–11). They were tempted to keep back a part of their offering of money and in giving way to that temptation they lied to the Holy Spirit. So it has gone on ever since: men (believers included) have sought to bargain with God, making solemn promises but ever hopeful of holding something back. But the New Covenant terms laid down by Jesus are not negotiable.

To be reconciled to Jesus means to be reconciled with one another, or it means nothing. As he laid down his life for us, so we are to lay down our lives for one another. Anything else grieves and resists the Holy Spirit. Jesus called this lifestyle, discipleship.

Discipleship brings dramatic and far-reaching change to the life of a true believer. It affects the deepest relationships and the most intimate. It calls for complete reorientation of priorities. Consider these descriptions of what true discipleship involves. These are all words of Jesus recorded in Luke 14:26–33.

- New Family Relationships: *"If anyone comes to me and does not hate his own father and mother and wife and children and brothers and sisters, yes, and even his own life he cannot be my disciple."*
- New Character: *"Whoever does not bear his own cross and come after me cannot be my disciple."*
- No Longer Reliant on Material Resources: *"So therefore, whoever of you does not renounce all that he has cannot be my disciple."*

This was the essence of Jesus' prophetic prayer. He foresaw his church as he prayed. Did he not say, *"I will build my church and the gates of hell shall not prevail against it"* (Matthew 16:18)?

But what happened to Jesus' great plan for his church?

From the very start, it became the focus for Satan's constant attack. Satan understood the source and power of "living water." His aim was to pollute it, to bring sickness and death to believers in place of life and healthy growth. By this means, he planned to destroy their testimony in the world.

Jesus said, *"If any man thirsts let him come to me and drink"* (John 7:37). The "living water" is personal and is only accessible to the one who truly thirsts for it. *"He who believes in me . . . out of his heart shall flow rivers of living water."* The result of receiving the "living water" is to become a source for others who thirst.

"This he said of the Holy Spirit." The "living water" is the activity of God in us, giving us life, dealing with our iniquity and flowing out from us, giving life to others. These results are interconnected; they exist together.

This godless world is filled with endemic hatred (manifested by tribalism, ethnicity, nationalism, and racism). The strategy of Jesus through the New Covenant was to confront it through a group of people from diverse races, cultures, and experiences, and united in a self-denying harmony of Spirit. They would be so united because they had drunk of the living water freely given by Jesus.

This would not primarily be a witness to the miraculous, external signs and wonders of God's own power over natural things, but to the demonstration of his divine power *within* each follower of Jesus Christ—a power that would transform his or her character into the very likeness of Jesus Christ.

Today, the visible church is riven by rivalry, hostility, and discord. Every denomination is riddled with disharmony, continual splits, disagreements and personality conflicts. So many individual churches present a religious picture to the world that is as unattractive as it is hypocritical. Have the gates of hell prevailed after all? Has the Holy Spirit gone from us?

Not yet!

In amongst all the confusion Jesus is still building his church. Each local expression of the church is made up of a motley collection of individuals, each at a different state of spiritual maturity: a veritable "raggle-taggle" that taxes the most dedicated pastor and pastoral team! This is the reason why there could never be a perfect church. Jesus knows that full well and does not expect it to be otherwise; but that does not mean that individual disciples may not develop into mature people, demonstrating the presence of Jesus within them and becoming overcomers. Indeed, these are the ones that will rule and reign with Christ in his coming kingdom. But they are as precious seed growing in a field of weeds; it is only the harvest that will fully reveal them.

Maturity does not come at the point of "salvation" but only through the process called sanctification (growing up). Jesus' prayer is still effective for his people but only as they deliberately make progress from childhood to spiritual adulthood.

When the people of the world recognize something different about true believers it is generally the unspoken testimony of their changed lives that is the first and most compelling witness to them. Where lives are not being changed, stagnation occurs and grave problems follow.

One of the significant features of the early chapters in the Book of Revelation is that in recognizing the condition of the churches Jesus lays the main responsibility at the feet of the leaders. As in the Old Testament the shepherds of his flock have enormous responsibility, and just as they failed, so most church leadership is failing. Jesus is not taken by surprise. He knew that the church down the ages would have a continual struggle with apostasy.

The ongoing struggle of the flesh against the spirit afflicts every believer. He is called to tread a narrow and hard path and there is no other way. Naturally the flesh does not want to be put to death by the spirit, but religion without an ongoing life change is empty: it has no substance. It remains tragically true that very few leaders have a testimony of a changed life; very few leaders today are a living witness to the truth of what they preach; and very few leaders understand the nature and purpose of discipleship. The call of the Lord through Paul in 2 Corinthians 7:1 is crystal clear: *"Therefore having these promises, beloved, let us cleanse ourselves from all filthiness of the flesh and spirit, and make holiness perfect in the fear of God."*

In cases where there is no determination to pursue sanctification, the only recourse is to substitute man-made activities for the spirit-led life. Paul called it *"holding the form of religion but denying the power of it"* (2 Timothy 3:5). All through history and up until today, men have sought signs and wonders for their own sake. *"An evil and adulterous generation seeks for a sign,"* said Jesus, according to Matthew 12:39.

Instead of promoting unity and changed lives, some ministers of churches have often majored on spectacular manifestations and sensational ministries, all too often identified with the same love of money evidenced by Ananias and Sapphira (Acts 5:1–11). This is the devil's work, for we know that ministry without spiritual maturity always brings chaos, and in consequence many Bible-loving Christians have become suspicious of what is referred to as "Signs and Wonders" ministry. Warnings like those given by Jesus in Matthew 7:21–23 should be sufficient to keep us on our toes.

But the ever-present danger is to "throw out the baby with the bathwater." The true church of Jesus has always manifested the power of the Holy Spirit through signs and wonders attending the proclamation of the Word. Indeed, without such ministry there can be no true maturity—a "spiritual Catch-22" situation!

The Bible tells us consistently that the last days will bring a time of special deception. False prophets, false teachers, false brethren, and even false "Christs" will abound and lead many astray. The uncomfortable truth is that they are here among us. These present days are those that will herald the coming of Jesus for his bride. Jesus warned that it would be an extremely testing time for the individual believer: a time of separating out those who love the truth and so have been changed by it, from those who are unchanged because they only pay lip service to it.

The issues we address are practical ones. They have nothing to do with denominations, structures, methods, and models of worship, but with evidence of God's presence in a church. Is Christ dwelling in his people by his Spirit? Is the risen, glorious, King of Kings living in my heart?

Such strange questions! Such a mystery! Yet the only evidence of the present rule and reign of the King is changed lives and the outflow of the "living water" to others (John 15:1–10).

This alone leads to the oneness Jesus prayed for. It increases with the maturity of the believer. It is based upon a shared oneness with Jesus and the Father. It changes the individual, it changes marriage relationships and life in the home, it changes families, and it changes churches, in that order. Unless we attain to this on earth here and now, we can *never* attain to it either in the millennial kingdom reign of Christ on earth or, indeed, in heaven itself.

Time to think. Time to act. *"The Spirit and the Bride say, 'Come!' And let him who hears say, 'Come!' And let him who is thirsty come. Let him who desires take the water of life without price . . . He who testifies to these things says, 'Surely I am coming soon.' Amen. Come, Lord Jesus"* (Revelation 22:17, 20).

THE CONQUEROR
A SON OF GOD GROWING TO MATURITY
A MANDATORY PROCESS THAT CHANGES US INTO THE LIKENESS OF CHRIST

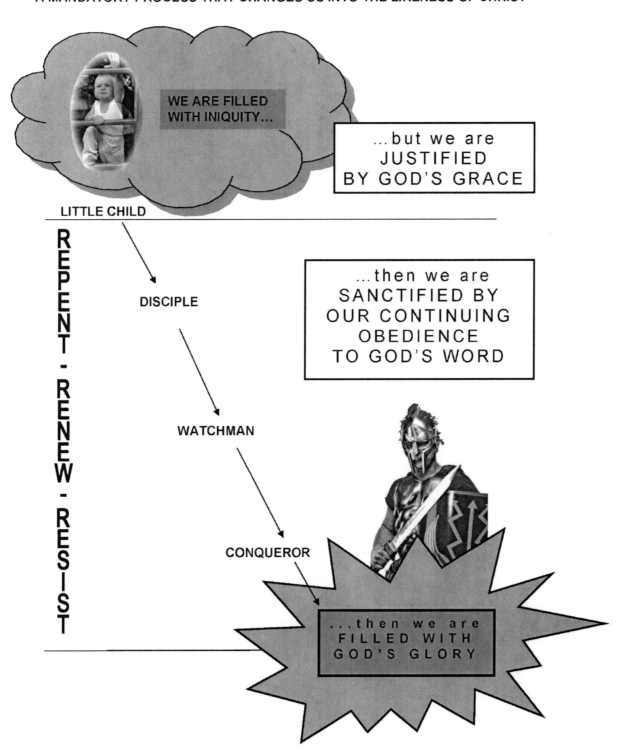

WE ARE FILLED WITH INIQUITY...

...but we are JUSTIFIED BY GOD'S GRACE

LITTLE CHILD

REPENT · RENEW · RESIST

DISCIPLE

...then we are SANCTIFIED BY OUR CONTINUING OBEDIENCE TO GOD'S WORD

WATCHMAN

CONQUEROR

...then we are FILLED WITH GOD'S GLORY

EPILOGUE:
"HERE I STAND!"

Historians tell us that Martin Luther famously declared these words when he made his historic break with the Church of Rome. For Luther, the sometimes fanciful and outright pagan doctrines of Rome were not the touchstone of truth; it could only be the plain teaching of the Bible! For him it was a matter of faith alone (*sola fide*), grace alone (*sola gratia*), and the Bible alone (*soli Scriptura*). When Luther took his stand, he also took his life in his hands. Such a stand will always carry great risk of opposition and attack from God's enemies outside the church establishment and within it.

The spiritual state of our country has always been close to my heart, but after fifteen years in London's East End, God sent us away to Africa and then to the USA. We had much to learn.

In the year 2002, my wife Juliet and I returned permanently to the UK after spending four years with a Southern Baptist Community Church in the USA. Over the last ten years, we have regularly returned from overseas to see our family and each time we have come home we observe changes that have taken place.

Some changes are practical—like the use of the Internet and increased traffic on the roads. But the changes I feel most are spiritual changes—changes difficult to quantify because they are "atmospheric," but typified by what is happening in the institutions of Parliament and the Church of England.

Today as Christians we face issues in public debate that would have been beyond belief only forty years ago. There are moral issues that have not previously arisen in the modern history of our country because everyone accepted what was good and what was evil because the Bible said so. Without the security of a generally received moral code, people have little idea of how to grapple with what is going on. Pressure groups demand liberty to follow their own ideas and soon begin to insist that society should embrace their practices as reasonable and normal behaviour. Without authoritative leadership from somewhere, society is adrift in a perilous and stormy sea. "Alternative lifestyles" have established such a pernicious and all-embracing grip on society wherein, despite the disastrous consequences we see all around us, it is impossible to fully document their dramatic effects upon our culture. Drugs, alcohol, fornication, pornography, hedonism, dishonesty, greed, and selfishness fuel family breakdown and moral turpitude.

Who is there to stand for God's order? In his day, Elijah was convinced that he was the only one left (1 Kings 19:10). I know how he felt. No one seems to be prepared to stick his neck out—even for the Lord's sake. Not only does the church as a body appear to be already compromised on most of these issues, but it is also trying to sanitise them to make them acceptable because it does not have the moral conviction to stand against them.

Are you challenged in your spirit to take your stand along with me?

For those of us who know the Scriptures, the dominating issues are rampant materialism (idolatry) and rampant promiscuity (immorality). They always go together. They are the same problems that afflicted the Amorites. Now it is the turn of the Western world; its iniquity is rapidly coming to its fullness just as Jesus promised it would, and judgement rides close behind.

Idolatry and immorality have always been with us, but now, biblical standards of behaviour that have long been publicly accepted are being set aside in favour of humanistic permissiveness. Our governments pass laws approving behaviour and practices that are objectionable to God, and our established churches, with no confidence in the Bible as the Word of God, are morally compromised and silent.

This is the work of the "Whore of Babylon" who represents the "alternative lifestyle" offered by the Spirit of Antichrist. The poisonous potion she offers to all to drink is the seductive lure of material gain with its ever-increasing international trade bringing more and more profits and higher Gross National Products for the nations. Without moral scruples to restrain them, men and women are in a position to indulge their appetites to the full. Nothing is forbidden.

"The kings of the earth have committed fornication with her" the Bible tells us (Revelation 17:2). It is a picture of gross spiritual immorality. The leaders of the nations want what she offers, as do their people. Everyone wants a piece of the action. The most successful win power and influence for themselves and their cronies. *"Thy merchants were the great men of the earth"* the Bible tells us (Revelation 18:23). This prophetic statement has never been truer than it is today. But like any prostitute, the temptress Babylon never delivers what she promises, for iniquity is never satisfied by material gain.

In fact, she has a hidden agenda. She is promoting the agenda of the Beast she rides upon. Babylon symbolises the Spirit of Antichrist. She is Satan's creature. Satan's spiritual agenda is to thwart God's purpose for mankind by substituting his own agenda so that he can rule. The revelation of our society as a whore is a picture of this purpose. It epitomises Israel's adultery with the world's culture. Its purpose is also to destroy Christian marriage and family because these are God-ordained demonstrations of his intentions for Christ and his bride, the church.

Destruction of marriage and family would achieve the elimination of both God's creation order for life and his image in the world. When God made man in his own image, *"male and female created he them"* (Genesis 1:27). This profound statement tells us of the image of God to be found in the unique relationship between a married man and woman who are filled with the Holy Spirit. If Satan can somehow undermine this special love relationship on the earth, then where can man look for a mature understanding of the Creator God who *is* love?

God's edict to the first married couple was, "go forth and multiply." The earth was to be peopled by a family who would become *his* family. Through the love and care of parents for their children, mankind would have an insight into the heart of God, their Creator, who longed so much for a family of his own. If Satan can reduce human procreation to an animal expression of lust between two unrelated individuals of any sex, then mankind can never understand the desire of God to people heaven with mature and pure children of his own.

The complete destruction of marriage and family is the target of the enemy. If these primary building blocks of God's order for life and society can be destroyed, then society will have fallen into irredeemable chaos.

The Western world has learned to take its Christian inheritance for granted, but that faltering inheritance, without the foundation of a living faith in Jesus the Messiah and Lord, is crashing down around it.

"Come out of her my people." So says Revelation 18:4–5. We have reached the last days. I know I should "come out of her," but how?

Yes, I must pray! Yes, I must go on being sanctified day by day! Yes, I must go on loving—even my enemies! But I must also declare "enough is enough"! I draw a line in the sand, publicly if possible. I will not join further in the process of decline.

I will not support or accept any person, party, or programme that seeks to further undermine marriage and the family in this country. It does not matter whether it is a spiritual, political, legal, or social matter, if this attack on the nuclear family goes any further I will regard myself as an alien in my own country and will refuse to undertake my civic responsibilities. If necessary I will refuse cooperation with the authorities and resist passively every exponent of such policies whether in the church or state, by all means at my disposal.

In the United Kingdom the Queen stands for the nation and its spiritual and moral values. Her Majesty the Queen accepts the title "Defender of the Faith." Although first awarded to Henry VIII for his fervent enthusiasm for Roman Catholicism, things changed dramatically when he broke with Rome, and the title came to be a trenchant claim to uphold the Protestant Reformed Faith. That is what "Defender of the Faith" still means today, although her understanding (and that of her family) appears to be sadly changed to mean *any* faith, however pagan! The Queen's Coronation Oath expressed unequivocal commitment to the truth of the Bible. Here it is:

Archbishop: *"Will you to the utmost of your power maintain the Laws of God, the true profession of the Gospel, and the Protestant Reformed Religion established by law? And will you maintain and preserve inviolably the settlement of the Church of England and the doctrine, worship, discipline, and government thereof, as by law established in England? And will you preserve unto the Bishops and Clergy of England, and to the churches there committed to their charge, all such rights and privileges, as by law do or shall appertain to them, or any of them?"*

Queen: *"All this I promise to do."* [Then laying her hand on the Bible on the Communion Table] *"The things I have here before promised, I will perform, and keep. So help me God."*

The Queen made that oath before God and the people of her realm. If she fails and her government fail to defend the biblical truth that is the basis of their authority, which centrally includes marriage and family as Christians have understood them to be for centuries past, then they have abrogated their God-given and self-sworn duty. They will have surrendered this land to the whore, Babylon, and thus prepared the way to receive the Antichrist as world ruler.

VITAL BIBLE REFERENCES TO HELP US TO STAND

We know who we are and who leads us. He has called us to be conquerors, and he is personally committed to us in every circumstance that we shall encounter. As we seek to obey him, he assures us that all things are working together for our good.

The presence of God
"The Spirit of truth . . . He dwells with you and will be in you . . . I will come to you" (John 14:17–18).

Reassurance to Jesus' disciples
"Lo, I am with you always, even unto the end of the age" (Matthew 28:20).

Jesus was tested too
"Then Jesus was led by the Spirit into the wilderness to be tempted by the devil" (Matthew 4:1).
"the Spirit drove him out into the wilderness" (Mark 1:12).

The secret of victory when tested
"The ruler of this world is coming, and he has nothing <u>in</u> me" (John 14:30).

Jesus sets the example
"Jesus, full of the Spirit . . . was led by the Spirit . . ." (Luke 4:1).

Disciples of Jesus are indwelt by the Holy Spirit
"He yearns jealously over the Holy Spirit he has made to dwell in us" (James 4:5).

Purpose
"The Spirit of the Lord is upon me, because he has anointed me to preach good news" (Luke 4:18).

His disciples received the promise of God for salvation and sanctification in the Upper Room
"He breathed on them and said receive Holy Spirit" (John 20:22).

Power comes for ministry
"Behold I send the promise of my Father upon you; but stay in the city, until you are clothed with power from on high" (Luke 24:49).

". . . he charged them not to depart from Jerusalem, but to wait for the promise of the Father . . . 'for John baptized with water, but before many days you shall be baptized with the Holy Spirit'" (Acts 1:4–5).

Paul, a chosen instrument, receives power to bear suffering for the ministry

"Go, for he is a chosen instrument of mine to carry my name before Gentiles and kings and the sons of Israel; for I will show him how much he must suffer for the sake of my name.' So Ananias departed and entered the house. And laying his hands on him he said, 'Brother Saul, the Lord Jesus . . . has sent me that you may regain your sight and be filled with the Holy Spirit.' Immediately something like scales fell from his eyes and he regained his sight. Then he rose and was baptized . . ." (Acts 9:15–18).

The promise of the Holy Spirit is to all

"While Peter was still saying this, the Holy Spirit fell on all who heard the word . . . they heard them speaking in tongues and extolling God . . . 'these people have received the Holy Spirit just as we have'" (Acts 10:44, 46–47).

Disciples of Jesus

We are to be "born of water and the Spirit" (John 3:5).

Persistence required!

"Ask . . . seek . . . knock . . . If you then, who are evil, know how to give good gifts to your children, how much more shall the heavenly Father give the Holy Spirit to those who ask him?" (Luke 11:9, 13).

Faith is necessary in everything

"Did you receive the Spirit by works of the law, or by hearing with faith? . . . Does he who supplies the Spirit to you and works miracles among you do so by works of the law, or by hearing with faith?" (Galatians 3:2, 5).

Love for true disciples

"God's love has been poured into our hearts through the Holy Spirit which has been given to us" (Romans 5:5).

Love flows out through spiritual gifts

"Make love your aim and earnestly desire the spiritual gifts, especially that you may prophesy" (1 Corinthians 14:1).

Sanctification = the inner struggle between *agape* and iniquity

"But I say, walk by the Spirit, and do not gratify the desires of the flesh. The desires of the flesh are against the Spirit and the desires of the Spirit are against the flesh; for these are opposed to each other, to prevent you from doing what you would. But if you are led by the Spirit you are not under the law" (Galatians 5:16–18). See also works of the flesh *versus* fruit of the Spirit (Galatians 5).

Ministry = the outer struggle: sons of God *versus* the ruler of this world

"For we do not wrestle against flesh and blood, but against principalities, against powers, against the rulers of the darkness of this age, against spiritual hosts of wickedness in the heavenly places" (Ephesians 6:12).

". . . you are strong, and the word of God abides in you, and you have overcome the wicked one" (1 John 2:14).

Witness of the Spirit—not by works or feelings!

"For all who are led by the Spirit of God are the sons of God . . . when we cry "Abba! Father!" it is the Spirit himself bearing witness with our spirit that we are children of God, and if children then heirs, heirs of God and fellow heirs with Christ, provided we suffer with him in order that we may also be glorified with him" (Romans 8:14–17).

Motivation determines fruit: Spirit *versus* flesh

"Do not be deceived; God is not mocked, for whatever a man sows that he will also reap. He who sows to his own flesh will from the flesh reap corruption; but he who sows to the Spirit will from the Spirit reap eternal life" (Galatians 6:7–8).

A new worship in the heart

"The time is coming when the true worshippers will worship the Father in Spirit and truth, for such the Father seeks to worship Him. God is Spirit and those who worship him must worship in spirit and truth" (John 4:23–24).

A new prayer intimacy

"Pray at all times in the Spirit" (Ephesians 6:18).

"For one who speaks in a tongue speaks not to men but to God; for no one understands him, but he utters mysteries in the Spirit . . . he who speaks in a tongue edifies himself . . . for if I pray in a tongue, my spirit prays but my mind is unfruitful" (1 Corinthians 14:2–4, 14).

A new praise

"I will sing with the Spirit and I will sing with the mind also" (1 Corinthians 14:15).

"Be filled with the Spirit, addressing one another in psalms and hymns and spiritual songs, singing and making melody to the Lord with all your heart" (Ephesians 5:18–19).

A new dimension of consciousness

"I know a man in Christ who fourteen years ago was caught up to the third heaven - whether in the body or out of the body I do not know, God knows. I know this man was caught up into Paradise—whether in the body or out of the body I do not know, God knows—and he heard things that cannot be told which man may not utter . . . And to keep me from being too elated by the abundance of revelation, a thorn was given me in the flesh, a messenger of Satan, to harass me, to keep me from being too elated" (2 Corinthians 12:2–5, 7).

"I was in the Spirit on the Lord's day" (Revelation 1:10).

"At once I was in the Spirit . . ." (Revelation 4:2).

9 781936 076772